Hg2 Madrid

A Hedonist's guide to
Madrid

Written by
Simon Hunter & Beverly Fearis

Photographed by
Ben Illis & Lyndon Douglas

A HEDONIST'S GUIDE TO MADRID
2nd edition

MANAGING DIRECTOR – Tremayne Carew Pole
MARKETING DIRECTOR – Sara Townsend
SERIES EDITOR – Catherine Blake
DESIGN – Katy Platt
MAPS – Richard Hale & Nick Randall
REPRO – ADP
PRINTER – Leo Paper
PUBLISHER – Filmer Ltd

Additional photography – Tremayne Carew Pole

Email – info@hg2.com
Website – www.hg2.com

Published in the United Kingdom in January 2009 by
Filmer Ltd
47 Filmer Road
London SW6 7JJ

ISBN – 978-1-905428-30-4

Hg2 Madrid

CONTENTS

How to…

A Hedonist's guide to Madrid is broken down into easy to use sections: Sleep, Eat, Drink, Snack, Party, Culture, Shop, Play and Info. In each section you'll find detailed reviews and photographs. At the front of the book is an introduction to the city and an overview map, followed by introductions to the five main areas and more detailed maps. On each of these maps the places we have featured are laid out by section, highlighted on the map with a symbol and a number. To find out about a particular place simply turn to the relevant section, where all entries are listed alphabetically. Alternatively, browse through a specific section (e.g. Eat) until you find a restaurant you like the look of. Surrounding your choice will be a coloured box — each colour refers to a particular area of the city. Simply turn to the relevant map to find the location.

Book your hotel on Hg2.com

We believe that the key to a great city break is choosing the right hotel. Our unique site now enables you to browse through our selection of hotels, using the interactive maps to give you a good feel for the area as well as the nearby restaurants, bars, sights, etc., before you book. Hg2 has formed partnerships with the hotels featured in our guide to bring them to readers at the lowest possible price. Our site now incorporates special offers from selected hotels, as well as a diary of interesting events taking place, 'Inspire Me'.

The concept

A Hedonist's guide to Madrid is designed to appeal to quirky, urbane and the incredibly stylish traveller. The kind of person interested in gourmet food, elegant hotels, hip clubs and seriously chic bars — someone who feels the need to explore, shop and pamper themselves away from the crowds.

We give you an insider's knowledge of Madrid; we want you to feel like an in-the-know local, and to take you to the most fashionable and hippest places in town to rub shoulders with the scenesters and glitterati alike.

Work so often rules our life, and weekends away are few and far between; when we do manage to break away we want to have as much fun and to relax as much as possible with the minimum amount of stress. This guide is all about maximizing time. The photographs of every place we feature help you to make a quick choice and fit in with your own style.

Unlike many other people we pride ourselves on our independence and our integrity. We eat in all the restaurants, drink in all the bars, and go wild in the nightclubs — all totally incognito. We charge no one for the privilege of appearing in the guide, and every place is reviewed and included at our discretion.

Cities are best enjoyed by soaking up the atmosphere: wander the streets, indulge in some retail therapy, re-energize yourself with a massage and then get ready to eat and party yourself into a stupor.

Madrid

If it's pure, unbridled hedonism you're looking for, then welcome to the world capital. Cruelly neglected in favour of its Catalan cousin Barcelona, Madrid is perhaps one of the finest cities in Europe to spend a weekend, week or even a whole month – indeed, many expats who come here to live temporarily end up staying for decades.

There's something incredibly Spanish about the city still – something that means you'll need to brush up on your language skills, as English is not widely spoken – which perhaps is to do with the fact that so many Madrileños can still afford to live in the centre, creating a vibrant mix of classes, ages and nationalities. Take Chueca, for example, where it's not uncommon to see suited professional types mingling with the gay crowd as well as the pensioners who have lived in the area for longer than they'd care to remember.

The compact size of the city is another plus, giving it the feel of a big town rather than a sprawling metropolis. Those who like to walk around to get the feel of their surroundings will be in their element in Madrid, as the proximity of the main attractions – not to mention the number of bars along the way – make this not only possible, but a joy in itself.

The people of the Spanish capital are friendly, welcoming and tolerant, and seem delighted that tourists choose to come and spend their holidays in the city, rather than begrudging their presence. Indeed, visitors would do well to study the habits of the Madrileño, as it's evident that they make for a contented existence.

For starters, much of everyday life here is lived out of the house and on the street, whether it's enjoying your morning coffee and croissant in the neighbourhood café, taking a long, leisurely business lunch in an upscale restaurant, or sharing tapas with friends in a bustling bar, which normally will be spilling onto the pavement outside.

Everything in Madrid happens just that bit later, leaving time to pack a whole lot in. Lunch is taken after 2pm, dinner not before 10pm and bedtime could well be sometime the next day. The nightlife in Madrid is legendary for its excesses, which date from the early 1980s and the days of the post-Franco cultural revolution, known as the *movida*. Revellers of all ages will be out on the streets at ungodly hours – in

fact, it's not uncommon to see families still up and about with infant children well into the wee small hours, making you wonder just when exactly these people get some shut-eye.

The city is to be enjoyed all year round, thanks to an average of nearly eight hours of sunshine ever day. Its location, atop a plateau, makes it the highest city in Europe, and means that an icy glacial air descends from the surrounding mountains into the city come winter. The warm sun, however, means this is no obstacle to a stroll, even in the coldest of weather. Summer heat is to be savoured, although in July and August the scorching sunshine can prove too much for the uninitiated.

But then, it's just a case of adjusting your habits – going out after dark and staying indoors around lunchtime. Indeed, most Madrileños clear out of the city come the summer months, meaning cheaper deals on hotel rooms and quieter streets. Be warned though: many bars and shops close for the whole month of August, so check ahead of time.

Whatever season you are here though, be ready to readjust your body clocks. Do as the Madrileños do and drink plenty of their rocket-fuel brand of coffee – you'll need it if you want to stand a chance of keeping up.

EL
VISO

4

SALAMANCA

TELLANA   LISTA

LETOS

7

MOS

PACIFICO

OCHA

EAT

5. La Broche
6. Le Marquis
7. Santelconi

PARTY

9. Moma56
10. Oz Teatro

CULTURE

11. Casa de Campo
12. Parque del buen
    Retiro

SLEEP

1. AC Santo Mauro
2. Hotel Hesperia
   Madrid
3. Intercontinental
   Castellana Madrid
4. Puerta de América

0   0.5   1km

Centro

Whether they love it or hate it, few Madrileños would disagree that the Gran Vía is one of the most emblematic avenues in Madrid. Running from Plaza España to Plaza Cibeles, it is always packed with pedestrians, traffic, noise and fumes, and is lined with flagship stores of global brands. In short, it is the Oxford Street of the Spanish capital.

The street itself was completed in 1921, some 20 years after work had officially begun to cut a swathe through the myriad streets that laid there before. The street has its share of history, the Telefónica building by Gran Vía Metro station having been used during the Civil War as a lookout post. Indeed, after the war it was officially renamed the Avenida de José Antonio Primero de Rivera, in honour of the founder of the falange. After the death of Franco, however, the name was changed back.

The grand, early 20th-century buildings are now home to offices and retail outlets, while a few notable hotels have sprung up, too, such as the Hotel de las Letras.

To the south of Gran Vía lies the Puerta del Sol, which is both the geographic and metaphorical centre of Spain. A plaque in front of the town hall building known as *kilometro cero* is the point from which all distances in the country are measured. This is where everyone heads come New Year's Eve, a crowd packing out the square to hear the chimes and watch the fireworks.

Mid-priced shops are to be found around the streets of Preciados and Carmen, while large chain stores, such as El Corte Inglés, Zara and Fnac, which sells CDs, books and DVDs, abound. Keep an eye out for smaller handicraft stores, which stock everything from Spanish nougat to intricately patterned fans, making this a good place to pick up an authentic gift from the city.

Head to the south-east of Sol to find the Plaza Santa Ana, a newly refurbished square that boasts some of the more pleasant terrace bars to be found in the city. The cafés and restaurants that line the square are worth popping into in wintertime, while the impressive ME Meliá hotel's terrace bar is a must any time of year.

Come night time, and the Calle Huertas, located just off the square, becomes a beer-soaked party street, filled with PRs thrusting flyers into your hand along with the offer of cheap shots. Perhaps best avoided then. During the day, however, the street – and those running parallel – make for a nice route down to the 'golden triangle' of art musuems: the Thyssen, Prado and Reina Sofía.

No visitor should miss a trip to the Plaza Mayor, the city's main square. Avoid the terrace bars though, unless you like being ripped off, and enjoy instead the regular markets and free concerts, normally coinciding with public holidays – this being Spain, there are plenty of those.

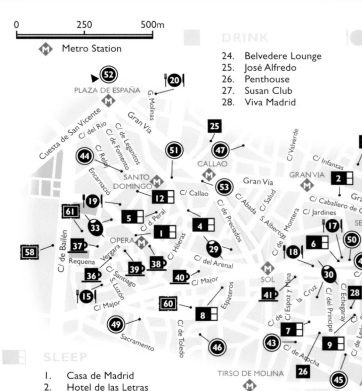

PLAZA DE ESPAÑA

Cuesta de San Vicente · C/ del Río · C/ de Fomento · Gran Vía · G Molinas · C/ de Leganitos · Encarnació · C/ Reloj

SANTO DOMINGO · **CALLAO** · Gran Vía · **GRAN VÍA** · C/ Valverde · C/ Infantas · C/ Caballero de G... · C/ Jardines · **SEV...** · Gran... · C/ de Peral · C/ Callao · C/ de Abada · S. Alberto · C/ Salud · C/ de Montera · C/ de Precia... · C/ de Hileras · C/ Hileras · **OPERA** · C/ de Bailén · Requena · Vergara · C/ del Arenal · C/ del Principe · C/ de León · C/ Echegaray · C/ de S. Santiago · S. Luzón · C/ Mayor · **SOL** · C/ Espoz y Mina · la Cruz · C/ Mayor · Espateros · C/ de la Cruz · C/ de Atocha · C/ de Toledo · Sacramento · **TIRSO DE MOLINA** · C/ de Sant...

Metro Station

0 · 250 · 500m

La Latina & The Old City

South of the Gran Vía, between the Plaza Mayor, the Palacio Real and San Francisco el Grande, lies the oldest part of Madrid, with the oldest part of all to be found between the Plaza de la Cebada, Plaza Mayor and the Palacio Real. This is the site of the medieval Muslim town, characterized by windy, hilly cobbled streets that are now home to exclusive restaurants and wine bars.

The La Latina area has become one of the most popular for all types of Madrileño, particularly on Sundays, when it seems that half the city has come out for an afternoon drink. The tattooed and pierced crowd occupy the squares, with litre bottles of beer in hand, while the affluent thirtysomethings bar hop enjoying mojitos, often spilling out onto the street along with their friends. Even stars like Javier Bardem are to be seen once in a while, enjoying a Sunday beer.

Head east on a Sunday morning, and you'll find the Rastro flea market, which stretches from the Plaza Cascorro right down Calle Ribera de

Curtidores. While you may be hard pushed to find something interesting to buy there, the atmosphere is unmissable, as is the chance to enjoy some tasty paella at one of the many bars along the route. Continue east to the immigrant neighbourhood of Lavapiés – a great

place for a cheap curry, but sometimes best avoided after dark due to the all too common muggings there.

West from Plaza Mayor is "Royal Madrid", which comprises the royal palace, the cathedral, the Teatro Real and the Campo del Moro Park, beyond which you'll find the wilderness of the Casa del Campo. Café de los Austrias and Café de Oriente make for refined places to enjoy a coffee, the latter having a beautiful terrace that overlooks the palace. Don't bother trying to spot any royals, however, as the building has not housed kings or queens since the abdication of Alfonso XIII in 1931. It is now a museum, and one of the most frequently visited sights in the city. The royals do make use of it from time to time, however, having chosen the palace as the venue for the royal wedding of Prince Felipe and Doña Letizia Ortiz back in 2004.

As you'd expect, this is one of the more touristy parts of Madrid, and food and drink here can be overpriced. But for the sheer sights and atmosphere, it's worth splashing out a bit – before heading back to La Latina, of course, to rejoin the debauchery.

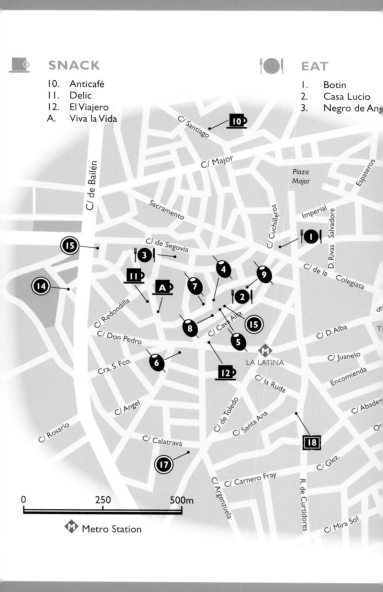

SNACK

10. Anticafé
11. Delic
12. El Viajero
A. Viva la Vida

EAT

1. Botin
2. Casa Lucio
3. Negro de An

C/ Santiago

C/ Major

Plaza
Major

Espateros

C/ de Bailén

Sacramento

Imperial

C/ Cuchilleros

D. Rivas Salvadore

C/ de Segovia

C/ de la   Colegiata

C/ Redondilla

C/ D.Alba

C/ Don Pedro

C/ Cava Alta

LA LATINA

C/ Juanelo

Cra. S. Fco.

C/ la Ruda

Encomienda

C/ Angel

C/ de Toledo

C/ Abade

C/ Rosario

C/ Santa Ana

C/ Calatrava

C/ Glez

C/ Carnero Fray

R. de Curdidores

C/ Argenzuela

C/ Mira Sol

0   250   500m

🅼 Metro Station

PARTY

13. Casa Patas
14. Corral de la Moreria
15. La Solea
16. Marula
17. Shoko

TAPAS

4. Almendro 13
5. El Tempranillo
6. Juana la Loca
7. La Carpanta
8. Lamiak
9. Txakoli

CULTURE

18. El Rastro

C/ de la Cruz
C/ del Prado
C/ de las Huertas
Relatores
C/ Sta. María
13
C/ de Magdalena
C/ Moratin
_INA
ANTÓN MARTÍN
C/ del Olmo
ús y María
C/ del Olivar
Avemaria
Tres
Peces
S. Carlos
Esperanza
aro
C/ de Lavapiés
C/ del
C/ de Zurita
C/ del Salitre
LAVAPIÉS
C/ del Amparo

Chueca & Malasaña

While they are only separated by a couple of streets, the neighbourhoods of Chueca and Malasaña couldn't be more different. What they do have in common, however, is great nightlife.

Chueca is arguably Europe's greatest gay quarter, having risen from a run-down neighbourhood full of junkies and street crime in just a matter of a decade or so. These days, the streets brim with cafés, bars, nightclubs and fashionable boutiques, with a level of tolerance toward the gay community that is not often seen.

Expect to see anyone there, from muscle Marys and bearded "bears", to young female shoppers seeking out bargain shoes. And be prepared for a wild night should you come here after dark, because the people round here like to party. The Gay Pride celebrations during late June and early July see the roof really come off, as the whole neighbourhood goes crazy.

In contrast, Malasaña is all about grungy, beer swilling kids, who bar

hop from lively venue to lively venue, taking the time to stop on the streets to knock back a few more. For this neighbourhood was the birthplace of the *móvida madrileña*, a cultural movement that saw the youth of the 1980s throw off the shackles of the dictatorship, and, led by figures such as film director Pedro Almodóvar, indulge in one big, long party.

Shoppers will enjoy the Calle Fuencarral, which is now a mix of one-off shops as well as all the coolest labels, while there are plenty of good places to get tapas and a sit-down meal, such as Lateral for the former, and Nina for the latter.

Between Fuencarral, Corredera Baja de San Pablo to the East and Gran Via lies an area until recently populated exclusively by prostitutes and addicts. Early in 2008 the TriBall Merchant's Association was founded to promote regeneration through art. While still sleazy on the side, TriBall is rapidly becoming one of the coolest districts in town and filling up with artists' salons, bars – like Jose y Alfredo – and hip boutiques.

Some of the back streets around Malasaña are best avoided late at night, but for the most part this is a part of town made for night time hedonism – just let the Madrileños show you how.

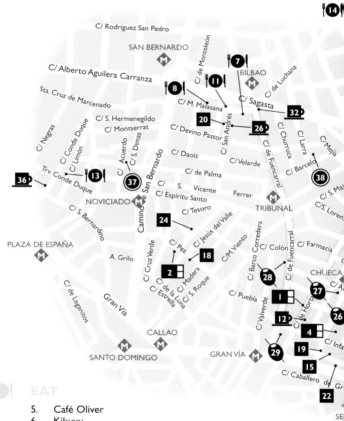

0   250   500m

Ⓜ Metro Station

10

LONSO MARTÍNEZ
Ⓜ

C/ Fernando El Santo

2

C/ Génova

30

C/ A. Galiano

C/ Sta. Teresa

Ⓜ COLÓN

C/ de Goya

C/ Fernando

16

15

6

C/ de Jorge Juan

31   23

C/ Bárbara Braganza

9

C/ Piamonte

17

5

C/ Almirante

C/ de Recoletos

Figueroa

34   21

C/ de Prim

33

C/ de Serrano

C/ del Barquillo

25

Marcos

12

Paseo de Recoletos

35

26

BANCO DE
Ⓜ ESPAÑA

C/ de Alcalá

Gran Vía

C/ de Alfonso XI

Salamanca

The swankiest part of Madrid, Salamanca is a grid of wide, elegant avenues lined with designer boutiques, luxury apartments and mansions, galleries and up-market restaurants.

It became the city's rich neighbourhood towards the end of the 19th century when the Marqués de Salamanca, a banker, politician and rogue known for his rather dubious business practices, built the first block of houses here, north-east of the city. His own house, on the Paseo de Recoletos, was the first in Madrid to have a flushing lavatory and Salamanca made sure these new developments had the same luxury. Soon other wealthy aristocrats realized the benefits of wider streets and new housing, compared with the narrow, musty streets of old Madrid, and flocked here in droves.

Today Salamanca remains home to Madrid's 'yuppies' and their offspring (*pijos* or *pijas*) who dress head-to-toe in designer clothes, wear sunglasses year-round, and drive top of the range sports cars.

Many of the city's most exclusive and stylish restaurants are to be found here, including Le Garage, Balzac and Matilda, while the area is also home to Madrid's most exclusive nightclubs, such as Moma56, where the flashy rides parked outside tell you a lot about the type of people inside.

While central Madrid is compact and manageable by foot, here in Salamanca the wide, long avenues mean you'll have to drive, or rely more on taxis to get from one venue to the next.

The roads can get quite busy and on the main shopping streets the pavements become thick with people, particularly between 6pm and the time most shops close, between 8 and 9pm.

Apart from its restaurants and clubs, the main reason to come to Salamanca is for its shopping. Top designer stores are mainly found on calles Jorge Juan, Ortega y Gasset, Serrano and Juan Bravo, while there are cheaper stores towards the east end of Calle Goya and on Calle Alcala. Private art galleries line Calle Claudio Coello, which, along with Serrano and Lagasca, is one of the oldest streets in Salamanca. They are narrower and the shops are smaller and closer together, making it a good area for browsing and window shopping.

To the far east of Salamanca is Madrid's famous bullfighting arena, Las Ventas, while to the west is its grand avenue, the Paseo de la

Castellana. Many of the city's largest and most luxurious business hotels – the Hotel Hesperia Madrid, Hotel Wellington and the Gran Meliá Fénix – are located along this wide thoroughfare, amid the plush office blocks of leading banks and insurance companies.

South of Salamanca is the beautiful Parque del Retiro, where Madrileños like to take a leisurely stroll all year round.

PARTY

25. Gabana 1800

DIEGO DE LEÓN

C/ de Francisco Silvela
C/ de Juan Bravo
C/ de Alcántara
C/ de Cartagena

C/ de José Ortega y Gasset
TA

C/ de Don Ramón de la Cruz

 MANUEL BECERRA

C/ de Alcalá

C/ de Goya

de Jorge Juan

DRINK

19. Balmoral
20. Geografic Club
21. Loft 39
22. Ramses

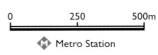

| 0 | 250 | 500m |

M Metro Station

SNACK

23. Jose Luiz
24. La Timba

SLEEP

1. AC Palacio del Retiro
2. Gran Hotel Velazquez
3. Gran Meliá Fénix
4. Hotel Adler
5. Hotel Wellington
6. Vincci Soma

EAT

7. Acquafredda
8. Le Dragon
9. Le Garage
10. Matilda
11. Montana
12. Mumbai Massala
13. Nicolas
14. Nilo
15. Ramses
16. Reche
17. Teatriz
18. Vincci Soma

SHOP

Calle de Jorge Juan 14 y 14 Bis
Calle de José Ortega y Gasset
Calle de Serrano

sleep...

It took a while, but Madrid has finally woken up to the phenomenon of the boutique hotel, and has taken to it with aplomb. The acme of this trend has to be the Puerta de América hotel (right), whose nine floors are all completely different and have been designed by architectural superstars such as Jean Nouvel and Richard Gluckman – eclectisism writ large.

There are interesting choices for all kinds of budgets, from the independent and charmingly quirky Hotel Abalu to the all out opulence of the ME Meliá. Hotels such as the Room Mate chain are squarely aiming for the young and affluent while the Hotel de las Letras draws in a mix of tourists and Spaniards alike, while keeping the night owls entertained with its excellent bar and terrace.

As well as all these newcomers, of course, there are some traditional and elegant hotels that are well worth a look. The most elegant of these, such as the Santo Mauro and the Orfila, are tucked away in quiet, leafy streets in the Chamberí area, or, like the Hotel Adler and Hotel Wellington, are to be found in elegant Salamanca.

Although these hotels are not bang in the centre, they are still only a short metro or taxi ride away from the heart of the city. Indeed, given that Madrid is so compact, location is not such a determining factor when picking a place as it may be elsewhere. Although if you're a light sleeper, it's probably best to avoid hotels around the Puerta del Sol and Gran Vía, as late-night noise will go on until the early hours.

The business district, along the Paseo de Castellana, is where you'll find the chains, such as the InterContinental and the Villa Magna, which cater for a corporate crowd during the week and then offer some great-value rates for weekend guests.

The best deals are to be found in August, when room prices can fall by up to 50 percent. But be aware that temperatures are soaring at this time of year – hence the lack of demand as everyone hightails it to the coast.

One final word of warning – as with other customer-facing businesses in Madrid, service is sometimes lacking when compared to other destinations, so

be prepared to complain should you find you are not treated in the way that the price tag on your room deserves.

Prices quoted here are per room per night, ranging from a standard double room in the low season to a suite in high season.

These hotels have been rated according to their style, location and atmosphere. 'Style' takes into account the furnishings and the appearance of the hotel inside and out. 'Atmosphere' considers the feel of the place: it might be super-stylish but nevertheless as inviting as a dentist's waiting room; again, it might be decorated like your granny's sitting room but still manage to generate a great ambience. 'Location' assesses how central and convenient the hotels are for shops, restaurants and tourist attractions.

Our top ten hotels in Madrid are:
1. AC Santo Mauro
2. Hotel Adler
3. ME Meliá
4. Puerta de América
5. Hotel Urban
6. Hotel Orfila
7. The Ritz
8. Vincci SoMa
9. Hotel Quo
10. Hotel Abalu

Our top five hotels for style are:
1. AC Santo Mauro
2. Puerta de América
3. Vincci SoMa
4. ME Meliá
5. The Ritz

Our top five hotels for atmosphere are:
1. AC Santo Mauro
2. Hotel Adler
3. Hohtel Orfila
4. Hotel Urban
5. ME Meliá

Our top five hotels for location are:
1. ME Meliá
2. AC Palacio del Retiro
3. Hotel Urban
4. Hotel Orfila
5. Hotel Quo

AC Palacio del Retiro, C/ Alfonso XII 14, Salamanca

Tel: 90 229 22 93 www.hotelacpalaciodelretiro.com
Rates: €236–985

This fabulous five-star hotel, which opened its doors in 2004, finds its home in a 1908 listed building, which looks out onto the Retiro park. Unlike many

modern hotels, whose small corridors and pokey rooms have been designed with profitability per square metre in mind, here the ceilings are high and the rooms are enormous, particularly in the case of the suites. The original classical splendour of the building has been carefully preserved, although modern touches – such as the backlit reception desk and carefully chosen furniture in the bar area – bring it suitably into the 21st century. Apart from the wonderful view of the park, the location makes it perfect for the sightseer, given its proximity to Madrid's 'golden triangle' of art museums.

Style 9, Atmosphere 9, Location 10

AC Santo Mauro, C/ Zurbano 36, Chamberí

Tel: 91 319 69 00 www.hotelacsantomauro.com
Rates: €279–1,070

A-list guests could be forgiven for barely venturing from the grounds of this classic palacette set in sumptuous gardens. High stuccoed ceilings and marble fireplaces provide a sense of regal grandeur, while cutting-edge modernity abounds in the bedrooms, which have been stylishly decorated in designer fabrics, furniture and soft chocolate and grey tones. This beautiful, elegant hotel is where the Beckhams stayed while they were searching for a permanent Madrid address. Need we say more? It's the former residence of the Marquis of Santo Mauro and is located in a quiet, leafy street in the wealthy Chamberí district where the Spanish nobility once lived. There are only 51 bedrooms, which is  surprising considering the vastness of the lobby and public areas. The small number of guests makes the hotel particularly intimate and exclusive, which no doubt appealed to David and Victoria. There's a fabulous garden and terrace restaurant, a grand library and an indoor pool. Rooms are modern, sleek and super-luxurious and have all that you'd expect from a top five-star hotel. The staff are charming and discreet, as is demanded.

Style 10, Atmosphere 10, Location 9

Casa de Madrid, C/ Arrieta, 2, Centro
Tel. 91 559 57 91 www.casademadrid.com
Rates: €220–390

Take no notice of some of the press that Casa de Madrid gets, which bills it as a 'Spanish version of the British Bed & Breakfast', because the experience here is so much more than that. Located on the third floor of an 18th-century building just next to the Teatro Real and the Palacio de Oriente, this unique hotel has just seven rooms – with names such as 'The Indian Room', 'The Greek Room' and 'The Damascus Suite' – all designed and decorated by the aristocratic Spanish owner. In fact, when you are staying here you may well feel more like you're in an apartment with maid service than in a hotel. Breakfast is served to you on silver platters, and is included in the

price – ask for any extras, however, and you may end up paying through the nose. While its location and decoration make it one of a kind, it can feel a touch gloomy at times, but still remains a fantastic base to explore the city from. A word of advice: opt for the airport transfer service they offer – you're unlikely to be able to find it easily otherwise.

Style 8, Atmosphere 6, Location 8

Gran Hotel Velázquez, C/ Velázquez 62, Salamanca
Tel: 91 575 28 00   www.hotelvelazquez.com
Rates: €150–400

Another of the old-style hotels in the Salamanca district, the four-star Gran Hotel Velázquez has light and cheery bedrooms with quaint pastel blue and

white flowery bed-covers and matching curtains. There are 143 rooms in all, including 72 suites that are super-spacious. The overall feel is rather formal and conservative during the week when the majority of guests are here for a conference or a meeting. However, the hotel takes on a more relaxed feel at weekends and has all the extras you'll need for a leisure break. There's even a gift shop and a hair salon. The bar, a popular meeting-place for the Salamanca crowd, has enough seating for everyone.

Style 8, Atmosphere 7, Location 9

Gran Meliá Fénix, C/ Hermosilla 2, Salamanca
Tel: 91 431 67 00   www.granmeliafenix.com
Rates: €170–1,220

Scarlet velvet *chaise longues*, ornate rugs, embroidered bedding and exquisite art all add to the elegant and refined feel of this hotel. The 225-room Gran Meliá Fénix occupies a National Heritage building that dates back to the

early 1950s, but underwent complete refurbishment in 2002. Club-class rooms and suites on the top floor include a wide private terrace with a hot tub for four, where breakfast can be served, and there is a separate concierge service and host of other added bonuses, all for a fraction more expense. Overlooking the flowing fountains of Plaza de Colón, the grand, circular lobby has a stunning stained-glass atrium decorated with enormous flower arrangements and punctuated by the dulcet sound of the in-house pianist. Staff are of the mature, well-experienced variety and the door staff are particularly cheerful. During the week, guests are predominantly here on business so the atmosphere can be rather formal, but at weekends the tourist arrivals lighten the mood. Maybe it's because they know they're only paying half as much as their corporate counterparts?

Style 8, Atmosphere 8, Location 9

Hostal Oxum, C/Hortaleza 31, 3rd Floor, Chueca

Tel: 664 72 32 41 www.hostaloxum.com
Rates: €59–99

Behind the rather unprepossessing interior of this crumbling 18th-century

mansion, right on the bustling Chueca mainstay of Calle Hortaleza, lies this oasis of simple but elegant calm. The friendly new owner has personally designed all the furnishings in the eight chic, minimalist rooms and had them made up to order. The standard rooms are somewhat on the small side, but at this price you really can't complain. All rooms have en-suite showers and every detail has been thought of – fully equipped kitchenette, Wi-Fi, i-Pod dock, air con and even a pet bed come as standard. Airport transfers, temporary gym membership, pay as you go Spanish mobile and a mini laptop also available by arrangement. Unusually for Madrid, a simple breakfast is included in the room rate, though you may prefer to stumble out to one of the many charming local cafés. For price and location, Hostal Oxum really can't be beaten.

Style 7, Atmosphere 7, Location 9

Hotel Abalu, C/ Pez 19, Malasaña

Tel: 91 531 47 44 www.hotelabalu.com
Rates: €100–350

The younger generation has seized the reigns at Hotel Abalu, with two
brothers taking over what once was their parents' hostel and refurbishing it
into an intriguing boutique hotel (indeed, mama y papa still lend a hand in
the café). Perfect for a naughty weekend away, the hotel's 15 rooms occupy

the ground and first floors of this quiet building, with some even lacking a
window, giving you a real feeling of being hidden away from the outside
world. The rooms have all been individually decorated by the brothers, who
have scoured the globe for furniture and accessories – all of which you can
purchase. The suites all have their own Apple Mac Minis with huge drop-
down projection screens, while electronic picture frames outside the rooms
display stills of what's inside (they're not CCTV, as many guests first think,
somewhat horrified). The only complaint would be the location, in Malasaña,
an area where certain streets are fine, but others are a little grim, with
prostitution and drug abuse a problem. That said, if you're prepared to brave
it, this quirky and original hotel is well worth a look.

Style 9, Atmosphere 9, Location 6

Hotel Adler, C/ Velázquez 33, Salamanca

Tel: 91 426 32 20 www.adlermadrid.com
Rates: €275–470

An absolute gem of an hotel in the heart of swanky Salamanca. The Adler is surrounded by designer shops and is only a two-minute walk from the Retiro Park, positioned on the corner of Velázquez and Goya, two of

Madrid's most distinguished streets. The sumptuous interior was designed by Pascua Ortega, who has created a smart, classic but contemporary look infused with the homeliness of an English country house. It is equipped with the most up-to-date technology, but has retained the grandeur of its 19th-century building. The 45 deluxe rooms have a classic modernity about them, painted in neutral tones mixed with a splash of colour and tartan. The restaurant serves first-class traditional Spanish meat and seafood dishes and there's a small, cosy bar for early evening drinks. Still privately owned, this five-star hotel has a warm, personal feel and the staff soon greet you by name.

Style 9, Atmosphere 10, Location 8/9

Hotel de las Letras, Gran Vía 11, Centro
Tel: 91 523 79 80   www.hoteldelasletras.com
Rates: €155–400

A literary theme pervades this hotel, which is located on the Gran Vía, Madrid's main thoroughfare. From the lobby and corridors to the rooms themselves, everywhere you look quotations from distinguished writers, in a selection of different languages, are emblazoned across the walls. Details from the early 20th-century building, in which this relative newcomer finds its home, have been carefully preserved, from the old lift shaft located by the new UV-lit elevators, to the impressive tiled entrance hall, also located beside the newer version. Of particular note among the 102 rooms are the

duplexes, which boast terraces and Jacuzzis, as well as stunning views of the centre of town. The bar downstairs attracts a cool crowd from outside the hotel, who come to enjoy a drink and the DJ sessions, while the attic bar is just as much of a draw thanks to its views and intimate size. An insider's tip: for some peace and quiet, head down to the library – it is little used and incredibly relaxing.

Style 8, Atmosphere 9, Location 8

Hotel Hesperia, Paseo de la Castellana 57, Chamberí

Tel: 91 210 88 00 www.hesperia-madrid.com
Rates: €175–290

Billed as Madrid's first five-star contemporary hotel and a member of the

exclusive 'Leading Hotels of the World' collection, this hotel set new standards in accommodation in the capital when it opened in 2000. Located in the financial and diplomatic area, it is, on weekdays, mainly a business hotel. The Hesperia's public areas were designed by Pascua Ortega, known for his work in the Teatro Real and the Hotel Adler. The overall look is Oriental chic (feng shui meets cutting-edge design). The 170 rooms and 34 suites are light, spacious and fitted out with all the latest mod-cons and luxuries, including Bvlgari products in the bathroom. The hotel is home to Santceloni (see EAT), one of Madrid's top restaurants, and an intimate Scotch bar serving more than 70 single-malt whiskies. Although there are only limited health facilities, guests get free access to the nearby Metropolitan, one of the city's most prestigious health clubs.

Style 9, Atmosphere 8, Location 8

Hotel Orfila, C/ Orfila 6, Salamanca

Tel: 91 702 77 00   www.hotelorfila.com
Rates: €225–655

A beautiful hotel that exudes charm and prestige, the Hotel Orfila is a member of the exclusive Relais & Chateaux group. This 19th-century palace,

in a leafy residential street in the Chamberí district, was converted to a hotel in the 1990s but still retains palatial ambitions. The lobby, with huge floral displays and *chaise longues*, has welcomed a plethora of international dignitaries and VIPs, but the highly professional staff charmingly treat all guests with equal reverence. And with only 32 rooms and 12 suites, the service is particularly personal. All of the rooms are different and exquisitely decorated; those with attic-style sloping ceilings have the most character. Equiped with hydro-massage baths, the usual array of high-tech gadgets are discreetly tucked away so they don't interfere with the traditional design. To top it off all guests are welcomed with a bottle of *cava*.

Style 9, Atmosphere 10, Location 9

Hotel Quo, C/ Sevilla 4, Centro
Tel: 91 532 90 49 www.hotelesquo.com
Rates: €96–217

Geared towards young, hip travellers, the Quo is for those who appreciate style and design but in a chilled-out, informal atmosphere. Located in the Puerta del Sol, right in the heart of the city, where, until recently, there was a distinct lack of stylish options. The corner building, originally 19th-century,

 has undergone a complete internal transformation, the overall look is homely meets contemporary, and the array of highly designed furniture is both comfortable and stylish. There are 61 bedrooms, six with balconies and one junior suite. All have a black and white colour scheme, with incredibly large beds. The hotel's restaurant follows the funky black and white theme, and is open for breakfast, lunch and dinner. The modern international menu meets modern behaviour as the refectory-style tables means that odds-on you'll be socializing with the other style-savvy guests. Ask for an interior room if you're a light sleeper, because the surrounding roads become party-central at the week-

end, and we all know how the Madrilenos like to party.

Style 9, Atmosphere 9, Location 9

Hotel Urban, Carrera de San Jerónimo 34, Centro
Tel: 91 787 77 70 www.derbyhotels.com
Rates: €185–275

Jordi Clos, the brains behind the Villa Real and Barcelona's Claris Hotel, has unleashed his wildest fantasies at the five-star Urban, sparing no expenses.

His amazing collection of Egyptian, African and Oriental art is generously spread around ultra-modern rooms and corridors bringing them alive. When you enter the hotel's atrium lobby you are greeted by huge tribal African shields, totem poles from Papua New Guinea and a backdrop of vast steel girders and glass rising up to an open canopy on the top floor. A winding thread of solid gold mosaic stairwell slices through translucent alabaster panels and various shades of granite sometimes cleverly exposing its rough side. A rooftop restaurant, deck and fitness area and pool offer vertiginous views of the city while the ground floor 'Glass Bar' and 'Europa Restaurant' are open to the public.

Style 9, Atmosphere 9, Location 9

Hotel Wellington, C/ Velázquez 8, Salamanca

Tel: 91 575 44 00   www.hotel-wellington.com
Rates: €135–580

One of only a handful of hotels in the city with an outdoor swimming pool, this traditional hotel is ideal in the height of the summer. The pool is open from mid-June to mid-September and is surrounded by a large sun terrace, while the new beauty spa looks out over it. The hotel was opened way back

in 1952, and the marble floors, chandeliers and lobby frescos have been maintained in good order. The Wellington was once one of Madrid's finest hotels but others have come a long way since and upped the competition. For those wanting to stay in-house there's a cosy English bar, a coffee shop, an à la carte Japanese restaurant (the Goizeko Wellington), a sushi bar (Kabuki), a sauna and a hairdresser. For those of a charitable disposition choose the 'Giving Room' option, where 10% of your bill goes to charity. Ideally located for shoppers in the middle of Salamanca, the hotel is within an easy totter of the city's finest haute-couture; for everyone else the Retiro Park and the 'golden triangle' of museums are a short walk away.

Style 8, Atmosphere 8, Location 9

InterContinental, Paseo de la Castellana 49, Chamberí

Tel: 91 700 73 00   www.madrid.intercontinental.com
Rates: €300–2,450

Primarily for business travellers, this huge 307-room hotel lends itself well to leisure stays at the weekends when rates fall dramatically. Although part of a large international chain the interior still retains character and charm. Some of the bedrooms might be a little chintzy, but they do have all the

necessary facilities; for a little bit extra upgrade to a club room where you'll have access to an exclusive club lounge. The huge, high-ceilinged lobby is a popular meeting-place, always bustling with people; while on the flipside the outdoor garden is a haven of tranquility The El Jardín restaurant is known to offer one of the best paella in town, alongside more traditional French and Spanish dishes. Bar 49, the cocktail lounge, is the perfect place to unwind with a drink, and if that doesn't do the trick the rooftop spa and fitness area offers numerous beauty treatments and oriental massages.

Style 8, Atmosphere 8, Location 8

ME Meliá, Plaza Santa Ana 14, Centro
Tel: 91 701 60 00 www.mebymelia.com
Rates: €199–2,299

If you go by Meliá's corporate website, then the majority of patrons at the ME are models lying around with their tops off. Unfortunately, the reality is somewhat more quotidian, but it is true that this is one of the more glamorous hotels to arrive on the scene in recent years. The building, which overlooks the newly remodelled Plaza Santa Ana, used to house the Tryp Reina Victoria, and indeed, until the deal fell through, very nearly became the Hard Rock Hotel. Meliá snapped it up and have done a great job of converting what was once 'the bullfighter's hotel' into a modern, luxury offering. Dark hardwood floors, rich linen sheets and state-of-the-art technology,

such as iPod docks, will please the most demanding of guests, while the excellent restaurant, The Midnight Rose, and rooftop bar, The Penthouse, provide plenty of on-site entertainment. The very efficient staff and unbeatable location top off this highly satisfactory experience.

Style 9, Atmosphere 9, Location 10

Posada del Peine, C/ Postas 17, Centro
Tel: 91 523 81 51   www.madridhotelposadadelpeine.com
Price: €90–128

Inaugurated in 2005, this boutique hotel finds its home in a 17th-century inn, and lays a very likely claim to be the oldest in the city. Located in a charming area of the city, just a stone's throw from the Plaza Mayor, the

four-star hotel has 71 rooms spread across four floors. But in contrast to the ascetic living spaces of the original *posada* (lodging) these rooms enjoy large, comfortable beds and hydro-massage showers, flat-screen TVs and minimalist decoration. A minor gripe would be the size of the rooms, which are a little small, but for a centrally located and historical hotel, it's great.

Style 7, Atmosphere 7, Location 8

Puerta de América, Avenida de América 41, Madrid
Tel: 91 744 54 00   www.puertaamerica.com
Rates: €159–750

The Puerta de América is a high-concept hotel, with every one of its 12 floors, as well as its bars and other public areas, designed by a star architect

– including Richard Gluckman, Norman Foster, Marc Jewson and Zaha Hadid. Therefore, you could visit literally 12 times and still be left wanting for another chance to take in the unique look of the floors and the rooms. However, its location is not great, being plonked way up town, just next to the A-2 motorway – although that does make it just a short hop to the airport. And from the outside the hotel leaves a lot to be desired, seemingly fashioned out of shiny red plastic, daubed with quotations. But once you're in, you'll most likely do everything you can to outfox the key system – which only lets you out of the lift on your floor – just so you can take in the stunning layout of each of the 12 floors.

Style 9, Atmosphere 8, Location 6

The Ritz, Plaza de la Lealtad 5, Centro
Tel: 91 701 67 67 www.ritz.es
Rates: €562–5,136

Perhaps Madrid's most famous hotel, and one of the original grand hotels of Europe, the Hotel Ritz was built on the orders of King Alfonso XIII who wanted a hotel to rival the Ritz in Paris. It opened in 1910 to much royal fanfare and is a fine example of *belle epoque* architecture. The impeccably trained staff make guests feel privileged to be here, but then maybe that's to be expected with a client list of such high calibre – they are used to dealing with the likes of George Bush, Tony Blair, Madonna, Brad Pitt and, er... the

Spice Girls. Pretty much every head of state and A-list celebrity has passed through the hotel's swing doors. The 137 rooms overlook the hotel's gardens, the Lealtad Square or the Prado; all have hand-made carpets, embroidered linens and original antiques as well as all necessary mod-cons. The lobby lounge is hugely popular for Sunday brunch and afternoon tea, and its terrace and gardens are a pleasant spot for some lunch or tapas. If you splash out on a suite, you'll get a free private airport transfer.

Style 9, Atmosphere 9, Location 9

Room Mate Alicia, C/ Prado 2, Centro
Tel: 91 389 60 95 www.room-matehotels.com
Rates: €117–320

As is the case with the other Room Mate hotels, Room Mate Alicia has an unbeatable location, on the attractive Plaza Santa Ana, also home to the

exclusive ME Meliá. From here you can easily access the city's art museums as well as the central Sol and Plaza Mayor areas. The architects have made great use of the views from the lobby, with huge windows letting the light stream into the minimalist, all-white space. Of the 34 rooms here, the duplex suites are of particular note, each equipped with its own mini-swimming pool out on the terrace, which look like large mosaic-tiled baths. The decoration and choice of furniture show impeccable taste on the part of designer Pascua Ortega, while the free Wi-Fi and other internet options available reflect the modernity of the hotel. It does get noisy around this area at night, however, so if you are a light sleeper make sure you let the staff know before they assign you your room.

Style 8, Atmosphere 8, Location 9

Room Mate Mario, C/ Campomanes 4, Centro
Tel: 91 548 85 48
Rates: €53–171

Room Mate Mario was the first of this ever-expanding chain of home-grown hotels, which have plumped for the interesting approach of personifying each establishment with its very own character. Mario, we are told, is 'a music composer and loves cinema', the idea being, of course, that if that's what you're into, you'll fit right in. The public the hotels are aiming for are the thirty-something, design-savvy crowd, who will enjoy the decoration from local luminary Tomás Alia, who has gone for black and white schemes for the bedrooms and a clever use of light throughout. The location of this particular branch couldn't be better, given that it is in a pretty and peaceful

street, which has the Ópera square on one side, and the Gran Vía on the other.

Style 8, Atmosphere 8, Location 9

Room Mate Óscar, Plaza Vázquez de Mella 12, Chueca
Tel: 91 701 11 73
Rates: €117–267

This is the most recent addition to the Room Mate chain, and, like the oth-

ers, presents us with a character to sum up the clientele: Óscar is an actor, 'whose friends could include Paz Vega', apparently. Let's hope she's hanging out at the bar then… The hotel itself looms quite imposingly on the Plaza Vázquez de Mella square, which is located just a stone's throw from the Gran Vía in Chueca.

Indeed, come Gay Pride week this is where a lot of the action takes place – meaning you should either avoid it at the end of June or book early, depending on whether you fancy trying to sleep amid one of the city's biggest parties. Designer Tomás Alia has turned his hand to the decoration, with suitably minimalist schemes in the bar and reception areas, and similar themes in the rooms. The incorporation of large pictures of muscular male backs within the decoration in some of the rooms may not be to everyone's taste, but it gives a general idea of the clientele the hotel is aiming for.

Style 8, Atmosphere 8, Location 9

Suite Prado, C/ Manuel Fernández y González 10, Centro

Tel: 91 420 23 18 www.suiteprado.com
Rates: €90–160

For those wanting a little more flexibility, this self-catering hotel is perfect.

Entirely made up of suites, with separate dining rooms and kitchens for those wanting to eat in, despite Madrid's amazing restaurants and cafés, many of which are just a short walk away. Simply and tastefully decorated in warm, pastel colours with generously-sized, wall-to-wall marble bathrooms. Some rooms are large enough to accommodate three people. If you stay here and choose to join the crowds at Viva Madrid, one of the city's liveliest bars, you only have to stumble a few steps home.

Style 7, Atmosphere 7, Location 8

Tryp Ambassador, Cuesta de Santo Domingo 5/7, Centro

Tel: 91 541 67 00 www.solmelia.com
Rates: €90–352

In the old palace of the Duques de Granada de Ega, the four-star Tryp

Ambassador has more character than the other Tryp hotels in Madrid. Retaining much of its original structure the interior has been refurbished in a lavish, traditional style, with elegant furniture, antiques and palms. There are 182 rooms, including 23 junior suites and three senior. Some are a little chintzy in style, but all the essential facilities are there. The hotel's main restaurant, El Invernadero, serves traditional Spanish cooking while the less formal Bar Entrepatios is perfect for something a little lighter. The highlight, however, is the delightful, covered winter garden, decorated with lights. Ideally located, just south of the Gran Via and close to the Royal Palace, the Ambassador is on a quiet road away from the hustle and bustle of this touristy part of the city.

Style 7, Atmosphere 7, Location 9

Villa Real, Plaza de las Cortes 10, Centro
Tel: 91 420 37 67 www.derbyhotels.com
Rates: €180–235

All the rooms have impressive views at this elegant, five-star hotel, located just a two-minute walk from the Prado and Retiro Park. The 115 rooms and suites are luxurious but a little dated, with parquet floors, root mahogany furniture and tan leather sofas. Although reasonably stylish they, are definitely not cutting edge. The 19 duplex suites have the beds raised on a platform to separate them from the sitting area, and some even have terrace balconies large enough to sit on. Bedrooms and public areas are decorated with valuable art, sculptures and antiques, adding to the overall feeling of grandeur. The Villa Real is part of the Derby Hotels chain, owned by Catalan

archaeologist Jordi Clos, who has chosen to display his private Roman mosaic collection around the hotel. The East 47 restaurant is adorned with Warhol prints and serves a full a la carte menu as well as tapas; for those wanting something a little less formal there's also a café and bar. Dogs are allowed, but unfortunately the hotel got rid of its gym and sauna, so fitness buffs might like to look elsewhere.

Style 8, Atmosphere 8, Location 8

Vinnci Centrum, C/ Cedaceros 4, Centro

Tel: 91 360 47 20   www.vinccihoteles.com
Rates: €100–170

This centrally located four-star hotel is a welcome addition to the Vinnci

chain, mostly thanks to it giving you access by foot to everything you'd want to see in the city. Sol is just a wander away, while in the other direction you'll find the Retiro park and the 'golden triangle' of art museums. There is an oriental feel to the décor, with futon-style beds, beige walls and dark wood, and the bathrooms are luxurious. That said, some of the rooms are a little small, and a good few look out onto an internal patio – good to keep the noise down, but a drawback in terms of a view. There's no car park either, so forget about this one if you've hired a motor.

Style 8, Atmosphere 7, Location 9

Vincci SoMa, C/ Goya 79, Salamanca
Tel: 91 435 75 45 www.vinccihoteles.com
Rates: €84–245

What started life as the fashionable Bauza hotel is now part of the Vinnci chain, but very little has been done to tamper with the original, retaining the cool, sleek décor. Pastel lime and berry cushions on cream sofas and beds decorate the airy parquet-floored Conranesque rooms and mini apart-ments, while the revamped restaurant provides a great place for lunchtime shoppers dropping in from one of Madrid's favourite shopping districts, Goya. There are 170 rooms and suites, with seven long-stay apartments.

Some feature large, decked terraces, but all have the requisite satellite TV, video games and spacious bathrooms. The Salamanca location is a little out of the tourist centre, but on the brightside the El Corte Inglés department store is just a two-minute walk away, and the Retiro park 10 minutes. The

Goya metro station will take you into the city centre in a matter of minutes.

Style 9, Atmosphere 8, Location 8

The Westin Palace, Plaza de las Cortes 7, Centro
Tel: 91 360 80 00   www.westinpalacemadrid.com
Rates: €225–455

Originally a palace commissioned by King Alfonso XIII in 1912, this hotel is a landmark in Madrid. A beautiful-ly ornate lobby, with a spectacular coloured glass-atrium, is worth checking out even if you don't end up staying here. The hotel has been renovated but has kept its palatial splendour. The most recent addition being an ultra-modern fitness centre with a sauna, massage or solarium. There are 465 rooms and suites, all with Westin's super-comfortable trademark 'Heavenly Bed'. The bar is an elegant spot for a coffee or cocktail, and with Spain's parliament buildings just across the road, you might find yourself standing next to a politician or two. The hotel is on the Plaza de las Cortes, right in the middle of Madrid's so-called 'golden triangle' of art – among the Prado, the Thyssen and the Reina Sofia.

Style 8, Atmosphere 8, Location 9

eat...

Food is the overriding passion of all Spaniards. Lunch with a group of locals, and before long the subject will turn to food – and stay there. How to prepare it, where to source it, where to enjoy it... nothing occupies the mind of a Madrileño like their daily bread.

Of course, King Jamón still reigns supreme in the Madrileño diet, so vegetarians should beware. It's often served as a starter, aperitif or within certain dishes, such as the ubiquitous potato croquettes. As well as their cured meats and sausages, Madrileños are also very fond of dishes Brits would normally baulk at, such as suckling pig, black pudding and tripe. With the exception of the latter (which no self-respecting person should consider bringing near their lips), it is worth overcoming culinary prejudices and giving everything a try.

Traditional dishes still dominate the menus of certain restaurants, ones that have been adapted from peasant recipes and are notable for their stunning flavours from the most simple combinations of pulses, vegetables and meats. Such cuisine is readily available in many of the finer eateries of the city, often given something of a modern twist by innovative chefs.

That said, Madrid has now woken up to international cuisine, too, and is particularly interested in sushi. Whether it's at dedicated restaurants such as Sushi 19, or as part of a varied menu, such as at the Midnight Rose (left), the raw stuff is big news here, as chefs take advantage of the wonderfully fresh produce flown in every day from all corners of the peninsula.

The influence of pioneers of molecular gastronomy, such as Ferran Adrià, has made itself felt too in Madrid, with disciples of his leaving their mark in outstanding eateries such as La Broche, whose nine-course tasting menu is an exercise in experimentation.

Wherever you decide to go and eat, make sure you don't arrive too early. Get to lunch for 2pm and for dinner at around 10pm, otherwise you'll be confronted by a shuttered restaurant. Dining is usually an experience to be savoured, too, so take your time. Most restaurants offer a wonderfully cheap set menu (one of the few good things to have survived from the Franco era), meaning you can enjoy some of the finer restaurants even if you're on a budget.

It's normally worth booking in advance for most of the restaurants listed, especially if you're going at the weekend. There's no hard and fast rule for tipping, but 10% is your best bet.

All the restaurants in this section are rated in terms of food, service and atmosphere. The price given is based on the cost of a three-course meal for one with half a bottle of wine.

55

Our top ten restaurants in Madrid are:
1. Santceloni
2. Memento
3. Zaranda
4. Le Garage
5. Midnight Rose
6. Laydown
7. La Broche
8. Don Pelayo
9. Olsen
10. Casa Lucio

Our top five restaurants for food are:
1. Santceloni
2. Zaranda
3. Memento
4. Don Pelayo
5. La Broche

Our top five restaurants for service are:
1. La Broche
2. Zaranda
3. Midnight Rose
4. Memento
5. Santceloni

Our top five restaurants for atmosphere are:
1. La Musa
2. Laydown
3. Midnight Rose
4. Nilo
5. Casa Lucio

19 Sushi Bar, C/ Salud 19, Centro

Tel: 91 524 05 71   www.19sushibar.com   €30

Open: lunch and dinner every weekday. Closed Sat lunchtime and all day Sun.

Sushi

Considering that Madrid is located slap-bang in the middle of the Iberian peninsula, it's surprising to learn that the city is the place to enjoy the best fish in the country, flown in from all corners daily to satiate Madrileños'

taste for the stuff. Indeed, Madrid is waking up to all kinds of cuisine, and the popularity of sushi is gaining pace. At 19 Sushi Bar you get a chance to sample the quality on offer, alongside American tourists looking for a fix or adventurous young Spaniards. The restaurant's tucked away location, just away from the bustle of Gran Vía, and its stylish décor, just add to its charms. The lunchtime menu offers a bit of everything, and is the more economical option, but it's worth splashing out to enjoy some fine *nigiri* and *maki*. A new branch, named 99 Sushi Bar, is now open at C/ Ponzano 99.

Food 7, Service 6, Atmosphere 7

Acquafredda, C/ Maldonado 15, Salamanca

Tel: 91 411 63 14

Open: daily, 9am–11pm   €24

Italian

Restaurateur Ignazio Deias is cornering the market in Madrid for Italian eateries, being the man behind La Piazzetta, Per Bacco!, Ma Tutti, and now Acquafredda. Tucked away in a side street near Metro Nuñez de Balboa,

Acquafredda encapsulates that most Madrileño of buzzwords: a *'multiespacios'*. All things to all men it's a place to have lunch, an Italian deli, a pastry shop and a wine merchants, all under one roof. The staff are 100%

Italian – as the dropping of aspirates attests – and are attentive and efficient. The décor leaves a bit to be desired, with gaudy red plastic adorning the deli area and the shop front, but the dining area itself is tastefully decked out with earthy flagstones and beige fittings. Well-heeled *señoras* and businessmen drop by to enjoy authentic Italian dishes off the lunch menu – but if it's dinner you're after, be sure to call and book in advance.

Food 8, Service 8, Atmosphere 6

Al Norte, C/ San Nicolás 8, Centro
Tel: 91 547 22 22
Open: 1.30–4pm, 8.45pm–midnight. Closed Sun evenings.   €40
Spanish

Hidden away in a narrow side street just behind the Palacio Real in an unassuming modern building is Al Norte, a very chic affair. Sedate businessmen and smart locals sink into the deep red velvet-covered banquettes to enjoy the Northern Spanish cuisine. Classic one-time peasant dishes are dressed up with sophisticated ingredients and a modern take. The menu, which changes monthly, makes the most of a traditional Spanish larder; however, it sometimes falls slightly short of the mark. The waiters glide around effortlessly, advising on the choice of fine wines and tempting dishes. Intended as a comfortable and fashionable retreat for the affluent locals, it won't win any

design awards but does enough to make you feel very grown-up. The food, the service and the stylish modern décor are the embodiment of simplicity and elegance.

Food 7, Service 8, Atmosphere 7

Botin, C/ los Cuchilleros 17, La Latina

Tel: 91 366 42 17   www.botin.es
Open: daily, 1–4pm, 8pm–midnight   €40
Spanish

If you don't mind squeezing in with hordes of eager tourists, check out this restaurant, which is famous for its listing in the *Guinness Book of Records* as the world's oldest. It dates back to 1725 and is a four-storey rambling den with narrow staircases, exposed beams and partly tiled walls, located just

around the back of the Plaza Mayor. Each floor has its own atmosphere, but the basement is the most popular. The specialties include roast suckling pig and lamb, and if it's not too frantic (which it probably will be) you might be able to persuade one of the helpful and pleasant waiters to show you the place where they're cooked. It's not a sight for the squeamish, however. This restaurant is a landmark, which means that you are likely to be surrounded by those in search of an 'authentic' experience, but it's worth it nonetheless.

Food 8, Service 9, Atmosphere 9

La Broche, C/ de Miguel Ángel 29, Chamberí

Tel: 91 399 3437   €150
Open: 2–3.30pm, 9–11.30pm. Closed Mon/Sat lunch, Sun and August.
Experimental

One of the stars of the Spanish culinary scene, Sergi Arola, won this minimalist, all-white restaurant its two Michelin stars. Since his abrupt departure, his protégé Ángel Palacios has taken over, maintaining Arola's passion for experimental cuisine that makes use of the famous foams and nitroge-

nized ingredients that caused such a stir when they were pioneered by El Bullí founder Ferrán Adrià (who, in turn, taught Arola all he knows). If you're looking for the cutting edge of creative cooking, you won't be disappointed here. The best plan is to opt for the tasting menu, which consists of 10 courses, allowing you to marvel at the immaculately presented miniature dishes that are served to you in quick succession – thankfully accompanied by a detailed explanation from the seemingly omnipresent waiter. As well as the more outlandish combinations, such as the langoustine carpaccio with broad beans, Catalan sausage and pork rind, there is also a nod to traditional Spanish dishes, with a mini sandwich *mixto* (cheese and ham sandwich) served as an appetiser, as well as a dedication to home-grown (or -reared) produce. It's not cheap, but it's certainly an experience.

Food 9, Service 10, Atmosphere 8

Café Oliver, C/ Almirante 12, Chueca

Tel: 91 521 73 79 www.cafeoliver.com
Open: daily, 1.30pm (11.30am Sun)–4pm, 9pm–midnight (1am Fri/Sat).
Closed Sundays & Mondays in August.   €36
International

Famous for its Sunday brunch, Café Oliver is rarely quiet at any time. Enthusiasm for the restaurant is fuelled by the credentials of the owners, who've worked with the likes of Conran. The décor is simple but stylish,

with a mixture of bare brick and painted walls, large mirrors, old-style advertisements and exposed beams. The restaurant is on a corner and has windows on two sides, making it bright, airy and cheery during the day. Friendly, good-looking and mostly English-speaking staff are dressed in black t-shirts and khaki aprons, adding to the place's New York vibe. The menu is international, with a set lunch that changes daily. Pastas and risottos are served in miniature saucepans, keeping them piping hot, but the most popular dish is the steak tartar. You can't book for brunch, which normally consists of fried eggs, bacon and orange juice, but bookings are recommended at all other times. After dinner, head downstairs to the Chivas Bar, a chilled out spot in an arched basement cave.

Food 8, Service 8, Atmosphere 8

Casa Lucio, C/ Cava Baja 35, La Latina
Tel: 91 365 32 52   www.casiolucio.es
Open: 1.15–4pm, 9–11.30pm. Closed for August and Saturday lunch.   €40
Spanish

Whether it's Hollywood film stars, visiting dignitaries from overseas or the King of Spain himself, they all head to Casa Lucio, a hotspot for the VIP

crowd located on the Cava Baja, the epicentre of traditional Madrileño cooking. To get the genuine experience, order the *huevos estrellados*, which literally means smashed eggs, and then tackle the suckling pig with chips. The extremely professional wait staff will ensure your wine glass runneth over at all times, and will guide you through the menu. The surroundings here are as rustic as the food, with low ceilings, exposed beams and led-light windows. Fellow diners will most likely be dressed up, with jackets and ties the norm, but you will still be OK should you turn up looking a little more casual. This restaurant is something of a Madrid institution, and shouldn't be missed.

Food 8, Service 9, Atmosphere 9

Don Pelayo, C/ Alcalá 33, Centro
Tel: 91 531 00 31
Open: 1.30–4pm, 8pm–midnight. Closed Sundays.   €55
Spanish

Entering Don Pelayo is almost like a trip into a secret Madrileño diner's
club, given that the actual restaurant itself is accessed through a door at the
back of an unassuming looking bar – the type that Madrid seems to specialize in. And indeed, once you're inside you'd be forgiven for thinking that

you'd stumbled upon a very run-of-the-mill restaurant, given the traditional
décor – all wood panelling and dusty looking paintings on the walls.
However, this is a classic Spanish dining experience, thanks to the excellent
wait staff, many of whom have worked there throughout the restaurants
two decades of existence, and its new chef. On the menu are classics of
Spanish fare all given the slightest twist, such as their potato croquettes
made with *cocido* broth – a modern combination of two age-old dishes. Be
sure to sample the glistening *jamón*, which will be cut from the joint by the
waiter as it is ordered. Look out for the live pianist, who plays on Friday and
Saturday nights bringing an extra touch of atmosphere.

Food 9, Service 9, Atmosphere 7

Le Dragon, C/ Gil de Santivañés 2, Salamanca

Tel: 91 435 66 69
Open: daily, 1.30–4pm, 8.30pm–midnight   €45
Chinese

Remove the tables from this labyrinthine restaurant and it could easily be a nightclub. Spread over two floors, everything is fashionably black, except for huge red dragons painted on the ceiling and red and blue light-boxes scattered among the tables. Staff are highly efficient and courteous but seem a tiny bit hassled by the huge number of diners demanding their

attention – something of a contrast from the feng shui principles employed in the decoration. The menu is crammed with traditional Chinese favourites, prepared in a lighter way to avoid leaving you too full. Food can come at slightly irregular intervals but the flavours more than make up for this. This is indeed a beautiful place worthy of the attention of Salamanca's beautiful people – a little slice of intimate New York transported to a quiet corner of Madrid.

Food 8, Service 8, Atmosphere 8

La Finca de Susana, C/ Arlabán 4, Centro

Tel: 91 429 7678 www.lafinca-restaurant.com
Open: daily, 1–4.30pm, 8.30pm–1.45am   €17
Mediterranean

The team behind La Finca de Susana have hit on a winning formula. The rock-bottom prices, speedy service and elegant surroundings – combined with the fact that you can't book in advance – mean that a queue forms at the door for those who deign to turn up later than 2pm. The

lunchtime menu – which includes a starter, main course, dessert, coffee and a drink – comes in at just €8.95, meaning the clientele ranges from smart businessmen and wealthy tourists, to scrimping students and smartly dressed pensioners. The quick turnover and rapid-fire service, courtesy of the team of highly efficient, mostly Filipino, staff, mean that the place is always rammed and enjoys a bustling atmosphere. For more of the same, there are several sister restaurants, such as La Gloria de Montera (C/ Caballero de Gracia 10), but this branch remains the firm favourite, thanks to the location, the light from the large bay windows and the sheer buzz of the place.

Food 7, Service 7, Atmosphere 8

Le Garage, C/ Valenzuela, 7, Salamanca
Tel: 91 522 61 97
Open: 1pm–1am Tues–Thurs; 5pm–2am Fri/Sat   €50
International

This recent addition to Madrid's high-end restaurants comes from the hands of two experienced French restaurateurs. That would go some way to explaining the French twang to the name, which is also no doubt influenced by the fact it is set in what was previously a car park. Now the interior is reminiscent of a New York loft-style. The first area you come

to is the square bar, complete with neon-tinted chandeliers, while the corridor that takes you through to the dining area at the rear is given over to a sushi bar, complete with chef toiling away with a sharp knife and sea-fresh produce. It's not all Japanese cuisine though, as the menu includes a slightly curious mix of dishes such as foie gras and langoustines flambéed in cognac. Impeccably dressed business folk swing by on weekdays, while the smart set from Salamanca are in evidence at the weekends.

Food 8, Service 9, Atmosphere 7

La Isla del Tesoro, C/ Manuela Malasaña 3, Malasaña

Tel: 91 593 14 40   www.isladeltesoro.net
Open: daily, 1.30pm–1am   €28
Vegetarian

One of a new generation of vegetarian restaurants in Madrid (they've been slow to catch on in this ham-loving city), La Isla del Tesoro serves healthy and tasty meals in a kitsch grotto-style setting. Its name translates as 'The Treasure Island', and so naturally the decoration adopts this theme. A fishing net hangs from the ceiling, adorned with fairy-lights, and a starfish hangs on the wall. An imaginative set-lunch menu is based on a different national cuisine each day – perhaps Greek, Indian, Moroccan, African or Spanish. It is great value and all dishes are designed to provide a complete and balanced meal. On the à la carte menu, the starters are almost the same price as main courses, but both are still reasonable. There's a menu in English and descriptions of some of the ingredients, for those who aren't dedicated followers of all things veggie. Unlike most, it doesn't close between lunch and dinner, so is popular for teas and snacks in the late afternoon.

Food 7, Service 7, Atmosphere 7

Kikuyu, C/ Doña Bárbara de Braganza 4, Chueca

Tel: 91 319 66 11

Open: 1.30–3.45pm, 9pm–midnight. Closed Sundays and holidays.   €37

Mediterranean

Simplicity and elegance are the watchwords here. Situated north of Chueca and east of Salamanca, this neighbourhood restaurant attracts the affluent locals time and time again. The dark, intimate room is the setting for some delicious Spanish/Mediterranean cuisine. *Carpaccios*, paellas and delicate fish dishes entice clients in, while a well-considered selection of wines complements the subtle

flavours of the food. At the front, a stainless-steel bar welcomes you, before you are led on to a darker middle room that is perfect for discreet conversations, while at the back is a further room with an occasional terrace. Kikuyu, as you might guess, was named after the Kenyan tribe, but the connection is somewhat tenuous as the owner fell in love with the name after watching the movie *Out of Africa*. This is a real neighbourhood treat, and you will need to book at weekends. Perfect for dinner before heading to some of Chueca's sophisticated bars.

Food 8, Service 8, Atmosphere 8

Laydown, Plaza de los Mostenses 9, Centro
Tel: 91 548 79 37   www.laydown.es
Open: 9.30pm–2am. Closed Mondays.   €35
International

The name says it all – forget the concept of sitting down at a table and chairs to eat, and get comfy on a pristine white mattress instead. That's the USP of Laydown, a restaurant that puts as much focus on its entertainment as it does on the food – which, by the way, is very good. The comfy beds,

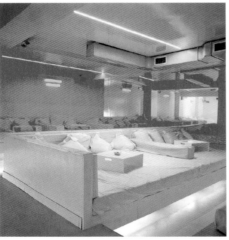

which are partitioned from the neighbours by oblong pillows, make this a good choice for a big group, or indeed for an intimate, semi-horizontal dining experience with your partner. Most nights there is some kind of music and/or a performance, which occasionally involves very scantily clad dancers – so perhaps avoid taking your grandma down. It should be noted that the alley leading to the restaurant may well rank up there as one of the dirtiest and ugliest in all of Madrid, but that's a small criticism for what is a one-of-a-kind experience in the city.

Food 8, Service 8, Atmosphere 9

Lhardy, Carrera de San Jerónimo 8, Centro

Tel: 91 521 3385 www.lhardy.com

Open: 1pm–3.30pm, 9–11.30pm. Closed Sun evenings.   €45

Spanish

Another Madrid institution, this restaurant has hosted politicians, dignitaries and royalty in the same elegant and formal surroundings since it opened in 1839. It has managed to retain its status to this day, largely as a

result of its signature dish, the *cocido madrileño*. It's Madrid's trademark stew, and was the everyday meal in the city's homes from the 17th until the mid-20th century. The type of meat used would vary depending on the family budget, and sometimes simply on what was available. Here, at Lhardy, you'll only get the best, of course. If you want a lighter bite to eat, there's a delightful and rather grand tapas bar and patisserie downstairs.

Food 8, Service 8, Atmosphere 8

Matilda, C/ Puigcerdá 14, Salamanca

Tel: 91 435 89 37 www.matildamadrid.com

Open: 1.30–4pm, 9pm–midnight. Closed Sundays.   €40

Fusion

True to its name, there's something delightfully feminine about this stylish restaurant, which is tucked away alongside some of Madrid's most exclusive shops in a pretty little side street. It's cool and modern, but the pink and purple furnishings and table settings, single-stem flowers in glass vases and brightly coloured luminous panel of photographs by Robert Garver give it a warmth and cosiness that could only be achieved with a woman's touch.

Indeed, it was designed by one of the restaurant's owners, Dana Galiana, who has won acclaim in the design world for her unique style. Tilted mirrors make this miniature restaurant (a former coach house) appear more spacious, and it almost doubles in size in the summer when you can reserve a table on a small garden terrace out the front. The food is described as 'modern fusion' and more than pleases the fashionable Serrano crowd. A great place for lunch on a summer's day or for a romantic dinner year-round.

Food 8, Service 8, Atmosphere 8

Le Marquis, Plaza de España 11, Centro
Tel: 91 541 33 93   www.lemarquis.es
Open: 2–4.30pm, 9pm–1.30am. Closed Mondays.   €40
International

This high-concept restaurant has taken the interesting theme of 'fetish' as its point of departure, mixing 18th-century French decoration with large-format photos of Marquis de Sade-style naughtiness. To add an extra touch of erotica, the chairs wear corsets and the tabletops are mirrored. The food is average, but the clientele are attracted more by the novelty of the venture than the fine dining – or lack thereof. Make sure you're looking cool and try your best to make it past the bouncer to enjoy the pole dancing area in the basement lounge. The particularly adventurous can give the pole a test-drive

themselves, helped along by the tunes supplied by local DJs from the Pacha stable.

Food 6, Service 7, Atmosphere 7

Memento, C/ Caracas 1, Chamberi

Tel: 91 448 99 58 www.restaurantememento.com
Open: 1.30–4.30pm, 8.30pm–midnight. Closed Sundays and Mondays.   €50
American

Run by American Karen Bell, who also acts as head chef, this fabulous restaurant brings some Californian cuisine to Madrid. Tucked away in a quiet part of Chamberí, the venue boasts stylish décor, nicely complemented by

the plate-glass front – perfect for people-watching as you enjoy your dinner. The food is spectacular, and each course is perfectly turned out – the attention to

71

detail that has gone in to the dining experience in Memento is evident with every bite. The romantic ambience makes it the ideal place for a dinner for two, but it will also serve well for a business lunch – ideally concluded with a tipple or two from the whisky menu.

Food 9, Service 9, Atmosphere 8

Midnight Rose, ME Meliá, Plaza de Santa Ana 14, Centro
Tel: 91 701 60 20
Open: daily, noon–4pm, 9pm–midnight   €60
International

Housed in the ultra-stylish surrounds of the ME Meliá, the Midnight Rose is the first venture in Spain from the Gerber brothers, and it doesn't disappoint. As you enter the restaurant, you may spot a nod to the hotel's

past as 'the bullfighters' hotel', thanks to the mounted taurine heads flanking the bar. The effort to conserve the original splendour of the building continues in the restaurant, although in a more subtle manner, thanks to interior designer Keith Hobbs (a man who counts George Clooney and Bono as clients), who has made good use of designer furniture to create a slightly retro feel. The menu comes stacked with surprises, such as the Oreo-biscuit appetisers, actually made of black olives and parmesan. Chef Jaime Renedo mixes up everything from pasta and *salmorejo* (tomato-style soup from Córdoba), to stunning sushi, which is all served by friendly and highly professional waiters. The place is very popular with the fashionista crowd, as well as visiting celebrities, who will all no doubt be hoping that the Gerbers open up another venue in the city sometime soon. Take a trip up the elevator to the terrace bar The Penthouse to end an evening of opulence.

Food 9, Service 9, Atmosphere 9

Montana, C/ Lagasca 5, Salamanca
Tel: 91 435 99 01
Open: 1.30–4pm, 8.30pm–2am. Closed Sundays. €50
Spanish

Small but incredibly chic, this restaurant is managed by Erika Feldmann and Ignacio González, who are around most nights making sure everything is

running to perfection (which it invariably will be). With only 10 or so tables to cater for, the pair and their staff manage to make you feel welcome and special, but without being too obtrusive. There's a surprisingly informal and cosy feel about the place, despite the glamorous clientele and the minimalist, rather sterile décor. There's just one velvet red curtain and one lone print; otherwise everything is whiter than white. But you don't need visual distractions. You'll be too busy enjoying the beautifully presented, delicious food. You can even watch it being prepared in the open-fronted kitchen. Good, solid Spanish dishes with a slight Oriental twist are created using only the best produce, some of which comes from Erika and Ignacio's farm near Toledo. You won't be disappointed.

Food 8, Service 9, Atmosphere 8

Mumbai Massala, C/ Recoletos 14, Salamanca

Tel: 91 435 71 94 www.mumbaimassala.com €50

Open: daily, 1.30pm (1pm Fri–Sun)–4pm, 9–11pm (midnight Fri/Sat)

Indian

It's unusual to find a decent Indian restaurant in Europe outside of the UK, so this will come as a pleasant surprise to anyone with a taste for all things

spicy. The menu has all the old favourites, and not only will they match up to your local curry house back home, they'll probably taste even better. Here, you'll get fabulous succulent chicken breast and sauces that aren't heavy and oily, making the whole curry experience healthier but just as packed with taste. The décor is refreshingly modern, but still retains that Indian touch. Hindu latticework, rainbow colours, gold and deep velvets create a theatrical, Bollywood feel, but all very tastefully and stylishly. The restaurant is divided into several areas, all with a slightly different feel. There's also a small bar, where you can lie back on cushions and loosen your belt after a good dinner. As with all good curry houses, they do take-away too.

Food 8, Service 8, Atmosphere 6

La Musa, Costanilla de San Andrés 12, La Latina

Tel: 91 354 02 55 www.lamusalatina.com

Open: daily, 10am–1am €30

Spanish

In the late 1990s a young team set up La Musa in Malasaña, creating a fun and funky restaurant that attracted a matching crowd. While that venue is still worth a visit, it's newer, bigger sister, La Musa Latina, is our preferred option of the two. Located in the incredibly popular La Latina district, La Musa Latina works on two levels. Upstairs is the restaurant, which serves

juicy meat dishes, hung from the skewer on which they were cooked, selected tapas and salads, all of which are perfect for sharing over a noisy evening with friends. Meanwhile, downstairs is the bar area, where satisfied patrons can wander down to enjoy a post-prandial long drink in pleasingly darkly lit surroundings. The wait staff are all too cool for school, but still provide a pleasantly friendly service, while the clientele range from twenty-somethings celebrating birth-days, to discerning forty-something couples.

Food 7, Service 8, Atmosphere 9

Negro de Anglona, C/ Segovia 13, La Latina
Tel: 91 366 37 53
Open: 2–4pm Sat–Sun, 9pm–1am (2am Fri/Sat) Mon–Sun   €40
Italian

Full of contradictions, Negro de Anglona is part stately home, part minimal-ist resto, and part Moët bar. The site itself was one of the first modern eateries to open its doors in Madrid in the 1980s, breaking the existing mould by serving Italian cuisine in a city that was just waking up from the constrains of a dictatorship. In fact, the history of the venue stretches even further back than that, the tunnel-like structure where diners now sit once being a passageway for adulterous royalty to move around the city unde-tected. The current set-up is perfect for a long evening, starting with a glass

of champers in the Moët bar, before you then head downstairs for dinner, and finally shuffle over to the bar for a few long drinks. Just be sure not to get lost in its labyrinthine layout.

Food 7, Service 8, Atmosphere 8

Nicolas, C/ Villalar 4, Salamanca

Tel: 91 431 77 37
Open: 1–4pm, 9pm–midnight. Closed Sunday evenings and August.   €38
Spanish

The fact that this restaurant is nearly always full on a week night is a testament to its popularity among its loyal clientele, who are almost exclusively Spanish. The locals are tempted here by the excellent menu, which includes

plenty of Madrileño favourites, using ingredients such as asparagus, truffles and carefully selected cuts of meat and fish. If offal dishes aren't your thing then you may want to steer clear (indeed, this is certainly not a place for vegetarians), but the more adventurous will be rewarded by the immaculate dishes, served by attentive waitstaff with superb attention to detail. The curved wood ceiling and low-slung, warm lamps lighting the tables bring a welcome touch of intimacy for diners, as well as a touch of modernity. Look out for Nicolas himself – he's the authoritative looking character who clearly knows his stuff.

Food 8, Service 8, Atmosphere 8

Nilo, C/ de José Ortega y Gasset 8, Salamanca

Tel: 91 431 60 60
Open: daily, 1.30–5pm, 9pm–midnight   €34
Modern Spanish/Mediterranean

This beautiful 19th-century residence, on one of the most prestigious streets in Salamanca, lends itself well to a restaurant conversion. The interior is refreshingly fun, with a mish-mash of designer furniture, leopard-skin throws and an assortment of kitsch chandeliers. Three dining rooms are separated by arches, the first room

doubling as a bar/chill-out area dominated by a huge bowl holding magnums of champagne. Ceilings are wonderfully ornate and deep windows look out over the wide, tree-lined street. The menu is modern Spanish/Mediterranean and is surprisingly good value. Despite its exclusive location, there's no stuffiness here, and you're more likely to be sitting next to casually dressed models, celebrities and media types than smartly dressed businessmen and their lacquered-haired wives.

Food 8, Service 9, Atmosphere 9

Nina, C/ Manuela Malasaña 10, Malasaña

Tel: 91 591 00 46 €28
Open: 1.30–4.30pm, 8.30pm–12.30am (1am Sat); 12.30–5.30pm Sun
Mediterranean

Restaurateur Nina, a somewhat formidable character, lends both her name
and her personality to this industrial, loft-style restaurant, which is more
Manhattan than Malasaña – the rather grungy, party-oriented quarter of the

city. That said,
the street
where the
restaurant is
located is
gradually
becoming
more up mar-
ket, thanks to
the addition
of several
high-end
restaurants
and a new

theatre. The venue itself attracts a relaxed and affluent thirty-something
crowd, who enjoy the large selection of Mediterranean dishes on offer in
the bare-brick, high-ceilinged surroundings. Be sure to keep an eye out for
Nina herself, who gives the impression that she runs the place with a
metaphorical rod of iron. Her bonhomie and attention to detail, however,
are always a welcome bonus for her clientele.

Food 8, Service 9, Atmosphere 8

Olsen, C/ del Prado 15, Centro

Tel: 91 429 36 59 www.olsenmadrid.com
Open: daily, 1–5pm, 8pm–2am (2.30am Fri/Sat) €35
Scandinavian

This wonderful restaurant is ostensibly Nordic, but also counts on a few
influences from Argentina, reflecting the provenance of the husband and
wife team behind the venture. Upon entering the long, narrow venue, the

well-stocked bar immediately catches your attention; as well it should given that it features an extensive selection of around 40 different vodkas. Indeed, some of the tempting dishes even come with a selection of vodka shots, served in attractive glasses on their own little tray. But aside from the complementary tipples, the food is fantastic – in particular the *blinis* and the marinated herring. The restaurant is very popular for its excellent brunch on Sundays, and also features a small but cool vodka lounge in the basement for a pre-club *copa*.

Food 8, Service 8, Atmosphere 9

Ottocento, C/ Libertad 16, Chueca
Tel: 91 521 69 04
Open: daily, 1.30–4pm, 9pm–midnight   €35
Argentinian/Italian

A relatively new addition to the Chueca culinary scene, Ottocento is yet more proof of the way in which this particular neighbourhood is becoming the epicentre of all things cool in the city. An Argentine team of restaurateurs took over what was once Carmencita, which, at 150 years old, was one of the oldest eateries in the city. They've done it respectfully, though, with an all-blue paint job, and a little inscription on one of the walls paying homage to the history of the venue. Expect Italian–Argentine fusion on the menu, and some very questionable cheesy Italian-themed music as a backdrop to your meal. The clientele consists of Chueca office workers and the artsy types who like to sniff out the next big thing in their 'hood.

Food 7, Service 8, Atmosphere 8

La Piazzeta, Plaza de Chueca 8, Chueca
Tel: 91 523 83 22
Open: daily, 1.30–4pm, 8pm–1am   €30
Italian

Plaza Chueca is a square in Madrid that constantly buzzes with activity.

The focal point of the gay quarter, it is home to fishmongers, fruit and veg shops, so-called 'old-man bars', gay bars, and now, thanks to La Piazzetta and La Dolce Piazzetta, two top-notch Italian eateries. La Piazzetta is a smart restaurant, complete with terrace, run by Ignazio Deias, the man behind the popular Boccondivino. The interior is a tasteful mix of beige, wood and mirrors, with plenty of natural light streaming in from the windows that

that face out onto the square. At lunchtimes the restaurant fills with office types, while at night it has more of a mixed crowd, reflecting the different tribes who frequent the area. The menu focuses on pastas and vegetables, and is complemented by an excellent wine list. If it's just a snack or a sweet treat you're after, then pop across the square to La Dolce Piazzetta, where you'll find a selection of sumptuous pastries to enjoy. A must for a late summer's evening, where you can enjoy this excellent food from the comfort of the terrace.

Food 8, Service 7, Atmosphere 8

Ramses, Plaza de Independencia 4, Salamanca
Tel: 91 435 16 66 www.ramseslife.com
Open: daily, noon–3am   €70
Mediterranean

Ramses is one of the latest high concept restaurants to arrive on the scene in Madrid, and has managed to achieve its aim of attracting the

fashionista and celebrity crowd. That comes in part from their rather snooty door policy for entrance to the bar, but also from the elaborate interior design by Philippe Starck. As the name may suggest, the restaurant has an archaeological theme, with the black walls daubed with note-book-style scribblings and drawings. If you're there to eat, you can enjoy the Bistro, with its Mediterranean menu, or just stop at the bar for a cocktail. The food is perhaps the least impressive thing here, though, failing to live up to the expectation created by the atmosphere and the glamorous crowd. If you want to be in one of the places to be seen, however, then you've discovered the right spot.

Food 6, Service 7, Atmosphere 8

Reche, C/ Don Ramón de la Cruz 49, Salamanca
Tel: 91 577 93 79
Open: 2–4pm, 9–11pm. Closed Sun and Mon evenings and August.   €40
Spanish

Another trendy, modern Spanish restaurant in Salamanca, the décor here is a bit too clinical, with grey and shrimp-pink office-style chairs and white walls. The restaurant is L-shaped, and the best tables are in the lower part of the L, at the back, round to the left. Here you will have full view of the

chefs through a glass window, in their whites, frantically chopping, stirring and adding the fancy, detailed touches to your *risotto*, steak or fish. The food is delicious and fabulously presented. Your fellow diners will be a mix of locals and those gourmets who have heard great things from their friends.

Food 9, Service 8, Atmosphere 7

Santceloni, Hotel Hesperia, Paseo de la Castellana 57, Chamberí
Tel: 91 210 88 40 www.restaurantesantceloni.com
Open: noon–4pm, 9–11pm. Closed Sat lunch, Sun and August.   €75
Fine dining

Madrid's reputation in the restaurant world went up a couple of notches when the Hotel Hesperia managed to secure the services of Santi Santamaria, famed for working his creative genius at the Recó de Can Fabes in Sant Celoni, Barcelona. Here, at Santceloni (a name that even the Madrileños struggle to pronounce), Santamaria uses the best local raw materials and, with attention to every intricate detail, mixes them together to conjure up delicious, first-rate dishes that quickly earned this restaurant its first Michelin star. The best way to experience his genius is to opt for the 10-course Menu Gastronomique for €125 per person, accompanied by one of the new generation of Catalan wines that feature on the wine list (one of the best in the city). Designed by Pascua Ortega, the restaurant is ultra-stylish, set out with the usual neutral beiges, creams and whites, and provides the perfect setting for Madrid's high-society set, as well as those who simply love great food.

Food 10, Service 9, Atmosphere 8

Teatriz, C/ Hermosilla 15, Salamanca
Tel: 91 577 53 79
Opens: daily, 1.30–4pm, 9pm–12.30am   €40
Italian/Mediterranean

This converted theatre was designed by Philippe Starck and, in true Starck style, the lavatories are as much of a design feat as the actual restaurant, with huge, marble Louis XIV basins, and stainless steel and mirror cubicles. The circular restaurant is dominated by a raised, gold-lit bar on the stage at one end, where moneyed Madrileños and in-the-know out-of-town-

ers gather for pre- and post-dinner drinks. Food is Mediterranean/Italian and surprisingly good value considering the Salamanca location and Starck credentials. Service is efficient if a little abrupt, but that's all part of the exclusive appeal. English menus are available for those struggling with the language. Dress up in your best togs and treat yourself, and don't forget to check out the loos.

Food 8, Service 6, Atmosphere 7

Toma, C/ Conde Duque 14, Malasaña
Tel: 91 547 49 96
Open: 2pm (1pm Sat/Sun)–4pm, 9pm–2am. Closed Mondays.   €25
Californian/Mediterranean

The name translates roughly as 'take that!' Take what, you might ask. Well, much like Madrid fave Memento (see page 71), what's on offer here is a lively and varied menu, reflecting

Californian and Mediterranean influences. Again, as at Memento, the owner/chef is American, so of course Sundays mean brunch. An added bonus is the low lighting, which, combined with the view of the Conde Duque cultural centre just across the street, make this a great venue for a romantic dinner for two. It's only small though, so best to book in advance, particularly if you want to squeeze in for the oversubscribed brunch. The restaurant has its faithful clients, made up of a mix of Americans and regular locals, and is a firm favourite in the neighbourhood.

Food 8, Service 8, Atmosphere 8

Vincci SoMa, C/ Goya 79, Salamanca

Tel: 91 435 75 45   www.vinccihotels.com
Open: daily, 1.30–4pm, 8.30–11pm   €65
Mediterranean

If you want to people-watch as you enjoy your lunch, then Vincci SoMa is the place to head, given that its first-floor location, within the swanky Vincci SoMa Hotel, provides you with a front row view to the Salamanca crowds as they spend their way around the neighbourhood. The bar area has an

ethnic feel to it, complete with bamboo details as well as the odd quirky touch, such as the slightly incongruous gumball machines, and is usually populated by foreign tourists and trendy media types that are staying in the hotel. In contrast, the restaurant itself is an essay in minimalism, the white walls and furnishings contrast with the black clad waiters who glide through the restaurant. Since the hotel was bought out by the Vincci chain, the menu has undergone somewhat of a transformation, focusing more on traditional Mediterranean meat and fish dishes than the fusion style that was evident before. The high standard remains, however, with a great value *degustación* menu for €65 per person, allowing you to sample everything.

Food 8, Service 8, Atmosphere 7

La Viuda Blanca, C/ Campomanes 6, Centro
Tel: 91 548 75 29 www.laviudablanca.com
Open: daily, 1.30–5pm, 9pm–3am   €34
Mediterranean

If that post-dinner amble to find a place to dance is one of your least favourite parts of the evening, then La Viuda Blanca may well be your dream

ticket. Located in a quiet street off Ópera, the restaurant finds its home in a courtyard with an impressive and dramatic glass roof. The décor is all white minimalism, with just the odd palm tree or ivy creeper distracting from the sleek lines, while the funky wait staff are kitted out in the seemingly ubiquitous all-black uniforms. The food is excellent, drawing its inspiration from a classical Mediterranean starting point but giving it a fresh twist. The menu comes already translated, making ordering a breeze, and ensuring you'll fit right in with the mix of well informed tourists and thirty-something regulars. A cheap lunchtime menu is an added bonus, as is a kid's menu if you should have little ones in tow. Once you've paid up, it's time to wander across to La Viuda Negra, the lounge bar complete with live DJ that adjoins the restaurant.

Food 8, Service 8, Atmosphere 8

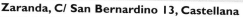

Zaranda, C/ San Bernardino 13, Castellana

Tel: 91 541 20 26 www.zaranda.es
Open: 1.45–3.30pm, 9–11.30pm Tues–Fri; 9–11.30pm Sat   €100
Fine dining

This superb restaurant started life near Plaza España, in a small venue with just 22 covers. However, once the work of chef Fernando Pérez Arellano earned a Michelin star, more room was needed to satisfy demand. Now located in the business district of the city, Zaranda continues to wow its diners, making use of seasonal produce to turn out immaculate dishes.

Arellano's wife is the experienced sommelier, overseeing a wine list as impressive as the menu. Thanks to its new home it attracts plenty of business types, but also a well-heeled and wise collection of loyal clients, who know that the culinary offerings will never disappoint. Opt for the Menu Arellano if you want to try a bit of everything, as the chef will offer up a selection of the finest dishes of the day in a tasting menu.

Food 10, Service 10, Atmosphere 7

drink...

Statistics say that Spain has one bar for every 143 inhabitants. Stroll around the streets of Madrid, and you'll quickly realise that that particular fact might just be true. Most common, perhaps, are the so-called 'old-man' bars, complete with fruit machine, smoky atmosphere and borderline alcoholics drinking brandy at 8am. These are not to everyone's taste, but they are nearly always guaranteed to serve fantastic coffee and tortilla, the potato omelette that is the staple of the Spanish diet.

But aside from these traditional haunts, there are plenty of smarter places to enjoy, in the company of those ultimate hedonists, the Madrileños.

Chueca boasts a few classics, such as Bar Cock, which was once a brothel in another life, and, legend has it, was connected by a tunnel to Museo Chicote, where Eva Gardner and Ernest Hemingway once hung out – don't leave here without checking out the pictures on the walls of famous patrons, past and present.

Newer options include Puro Placer, where you can choose a Cuban cigar to

accompany your beverage (no one takes any notice of the anti-smoking laws in Madrid), and José y Alfredo, which is very popular with cinema types. Restaurant Ølsen provides a great basement lounge for all kinds of vodka cocktails, while Nietzsche is an amusing place where you can catch performance art.

If it's a wilder, more beery atmosphere you're looking for, then Malasaña should do the trick – there you can knock back shots in noisy bars such as Cafeína. And should you fancy something more swanky, head up to the top of the ME Meliá hotel to enjoy The Penthouse terrace (left), where you can enjoy stunning views of the city's rooftops while sipping at a cocktail or three.

Drinking is an integral part of Spanish culture, but drunkenness is not. That means you'll see little of the yobbish behaviour so common in the UK come closing time – something helped by the fact that closing time is much, much later here, with most bars chucking out at 3.30am.

Thursday through Saturday nights are the best times to head out, but make sure you do so late. No one else will be getting their collective groove on until at least 11pm, so have a late dinner and a nap, and then get ready to explore. There is something to be said for a Sunday night jaunt, when the few places that are open will still be busy.

The selection of bars listed here is a mix of traditional, funky and sophisticated, and all of them are within easy reach of the city centre. Remember, however, in Madrid there is a thin line between bar, café and restaurant, so many of the venues included in Eat, Tapas and Café may also make a great place to have a drink.

Areia, C/ Hortaleza 92, Chueca

Tel: 91 310 03 07 www.areiachillout.com
Open: daily, 12.30pm–3am (3.30am Fri/Sat)

When Areia, dubbed a 'colonial chill out bar' (whatever that might be), first appeared, it became one of the hippest spots in the city having been born from a very uncool Irish pub. The tattooed and pierced crowd flocked here, attracted by the four-poster bed at the back and the sofas-come-beds in the

front. But very quickly the place got a little too cool for its own good and now attracts a mix of the *pijo* set, alongside the hipsters that made it popular in the first place. As well as freshly ground mojitos, you can choose from a selection of cocktails, teas and cakes, and even grab a brunch come Sunday. The décor gives the dimly lit interior a North African feel, while live DJs provide a chilled-out soundtrack to the evening. The only complaint is the volume of said music, as noise restrictions mean that at peak times it is barely audible above all the hub-bub.

Balmoral, C/ Hermosilla 10, Salamanca

Tel: 91 431 41 33
Open: noon–1am. Closed Sundays.

Entirely different from any other bar in Madrid, Balmoral is formal but unstuffy, and with its grand fireplace and range of fine whiskies, you would be forgiven for thinking you were in a remote castle in the Scottish highlands. It gets busy in two shifts – firstly from 7.30pm to 9pm with after-work drinkers and shoppers, and then with the up-market Salamanca regu-

lars who arrive late for the last of the night. Passers-by are warmly welcomed and this is a great spot for a coffee or digestif after a meal in one of Salamanca's smarter restaurants. The refined and civilized atmosphere means there are no queues at the bar, no music and plenty of chairs to go around. Balmoral first opened in 1955 and hasn't changed much since. In its heyday (in 1987/88) it was voted Best Bar in Europe by *Newsweek* magazine.

Bar Cock, C/ Reina 16, Centro
Tel: 91 532 28 26
Open: daily, 8pm–3am

Once you've had a little snigger at the name, it's worth checking out this long-established cocktail bar, which according to legend, was once a brothel

connected by a tunnel to Museo Chicote on Gran Vía. The rather ornate furnishing inside belies the long history of the venue, and the very serious staff only add to the feeling that you're in a place where professional drinking is encouraged. Indeed, dare to take your camera out and you'll be politely but firmly told that you don't do that sort of thing around here. In contrast to the style and the ambience of the place, the DJ roster is surprising, with somewhat incongruous electro sessions the order of the day. The prices are high, but this is after all a Madrid institution.

Belvedere Lounge, Ølsen, C/ Prado 15, Centro
Tel: 91 429 36 59   www.olsenmadrid.com
Open: 10pm–2.30am Fri–Sat

As if opening one of the best restaurants to arrive in the city in recent years wasn't enough, the team behind Ølsen have also deigned to bring us one of the coolest lounge bars, too. Located in the basement of the eatery,

the Belvedere Lounge is a comfortingly intimate cocktail bar, which specializes in vodka drinks. Weekend nights sees a DJ in session, meaning you can bust a move or two before heading off to a club. Ample seating also gives you the chance to just chill and admire the pretty people, if that's what you fancy.

Bristol Bar, C/ Almirante 20, Chueca
Tel: 91 522 45 68 www.bristolbar.es
Open: 9am–12.30am. Closed Sundays.

Madrid, like most other cities in the world, has its fair share of Irish pubs,

which are great for two things: watching sports events and meeting fellow visitors to a city. If, however, their often grimy atmosphere is a turn off for you, then head to Bristol Bar instead, a British-themed establishment where you're bound to run into more than a few expats as well as a crowd of smart Spaniards. A large picture of Queen Victoria keeps an eye on the proceedings in the front area of the bar, where you can order a G&T made with whichever brand of gin you fancy – and there are plenty on offer. In the back there's a restaurant serving British and American dishes, including a decent Sunday brunch.

Cafeína, C/ del Pez 18, Malasaña

Tel: 91 522 03 31
Open: 3pm–2am (3am Fri/Sat). Closed Sundays.

The Calle Pez, or Fish Street, is packed with inviting little bars, without the streets being as hectic – or as beer soaked – as the more central part of Malasaña. Cafeina is one of the neighbourhood favourites for those looking for a cool place to begin a long night out. If it's too crowded on the ground level, nip down to the basement to see if any of the chairs and sofas are still free – but if you're there at the weekend, chances are they won't be. Should you come by during the daytime, the bay windows make the venue a great place to stare into space and watch the locals go about their daily grind, with a soundtrack of jazz and laid-back hip hop to keep your head nodding.

Del Diego, C/ Reina 12, Centro

Tel: 91 522 75 44
Open: 7pm–3am (3.30am Fri/Sat). Closed Sundays.

You'll be spellbound by the skill and speed of the barmen in this tiny, low-key and refreshingly unpretentious cocktail bar. They look as though they've been mixing cocktails so long they could do it in their sleep, and while they're crushing ice and adding salt or sugar in a blur of activity, they'll still

be taking orders from whoever's next to walk through the door. All of the 50 plus cocktails on the menu are around €7.50, although the house special, Del Diego (vodka, kirsch, peach, lemon and soda water), is a little disappointing. You can opt for table service at one of the few tables, but it's much more fun to stand at the bar – if there's room. The décor is uninspiring but it doesn't matter – the cocktails take centre-stage here.

EO Chivas Lounge, C/ Almirante 1, Chueca
Tel: 91 521 73 79 www.cafeoliver.com
Open: 10pm–3am. Closed Sundays and Mondays.

Located in the tunnel-shaped basement of Café Oliver, one of Chueca's most popular restaurants, the EO Chivas Lounge has a ready-made clientele of pre- and post-dinner drinkers. It has, however, established a loyal following in its own right, thanks to its classic surroundings, superb cocktails and funky vibes.

Earlier in the week, you'll find elegantly dressed couples sipping champagne and making small-talk on suede couches, then from Thursday to Saturday DJs pick up the tempo with some choice tunes. Gorgeous staff grace the bar, expertly mixing cocktails and adding to the overall chic, up-market feel. Whether you're eating upstairs or not, this place is one for a special occasion.

Geografic Club, C/ Alcala 141, Salamanca
Tel: 91 578 08 62
Open: daily, 1pm–1.30am (3.30am Fri–Sat)

There aren't many bars in Barrio Salamanca, let alone decent ones, so it's not surprising that the Geografic is packed day and night. It's a vast, three-storey space with an enormous and beautiful stained-glass doorway and sky-light through which the sun seeps during the day. As the name suggests, the bar is testament to colonial exploration, with posters and artefacts from the far corners of the world, including African masks, snow shoes and the first hot-air balloon to land on Spanish soil. The chic Salamanca crowd pours in after work, staying until late in the evening. The reasonably priced restaurant

upstairs is hardly ever busy as drinkers prefer to munch on the tapas, such as fried vegetables and deep-fried goat's cheese, at the bar. The chocolate brownies are hugely popular with the late-night coffee crowd.

José Alfredo, C/ Silva 22, Centro

Tel: 91 521 49 60
Open: 7.30pm–3am. Closed Sundays.

A recent trend in Madrid has seen some very cool bars spring up in old-fashioned venues. Along with Demode, José Alfredo is one of the best of its kind, serving up a selection of 26 different cocktails along with the *copas* (insanely strong long drinks) so integral to a Spanish night out. The bar itself tends to be quite busy, so head towards the back where you'll find a cosy mirrored room, complete with sofas. Stake it out for a little while and

pounce as soon as a seat comes up. The action is presided over by some very cool, pierced and tattooed wait staff, who, while they may look a little intimidating, are actually very friendly and courteous. Keep your eyes peeled for the odd Almodóvar starlet, as the venue is popular with movers and shakers in the domestic film industry.

Loft 39, C/ Velázquez 39, Salamanca
Tel: 91 432 43 86   www.restauranteloft39.com
Open: daily, 11am–3am

If you didn't know where to look, you might well walk past the plain glass sliding doors that serve as the entrance to Loft 39, a lounge bar with adjoining restaurant that's located on one of Madrid's more exclusive streets. Once inside, either take the lift or the stairs up to the bar itself, which sports rather ornate décor complete with stained glass windows. Opt for a sofa if there's one free rather than the bar stools, which look (and feel) as if

they have been fashioned out of old shopping trolleys. Everything stocked behind the bar smacks of quality, whether it's the fresh fruit that goes in to all of their cocktails – barring the few that require Monin syrups – or the wide range of reserve spirits. Generously proportioned wallets are the only thing that the mixed crowd has in common, with a range of ages and fashion styles in evidence. Perhaps the only gripe is that the open air courtyard, so temptingly visible through the window, is not accessible to patrons due to noise restrictions. But that's a small complaint when you take into account the quality of the cocktails on offer and the exclusive vibe.

Museo Chicote, C/ Gran Vía 12, Centro

Tel: 91 523 67 37 www.museo-chicote.com
Open: 8am–3am. Closed Sundays.

Located on the Gran Vía, Chicote is a world-famous art deco bar, thanks to its famous patrons, not least one E. Hemingway, who did plenty of war reporting from here. For evidence of its star draw, look no further than the walls, which are plastered with pictures of all sorts of Hollywood names as

well as domestic celebs when they've come to call. During the day it's a great place to grab a coffee or an early beer, while at night a carefully picked line-up of DJs provides a lounge soundtrack to your evening drinks.

Neitzsche, C/ Doctor Fourquet 12, Lavapies

Tel: 91 506 11 41 www.nietzsche.com.es
Open: 6pm–1.30am (3am Fri/Sat). Closed Sundays.

Given its location, tucked away between the Reina Sofía art museum and the bohemian neighbourhood of Lavapiés, it's no surprise that Neitzsche attracts artsy types. Young movers and shakers on the local scene flock to the place, hanging around smoking 'jazz cigarettes' outside the venue and hitting the booze on the inside. They come down to enjoy the live music acts that often feature, as well as some truly odd performance art. Projection screens in the middle of the bar add to the overall surreal feel of the place, while the comfy sofas that line the walls throughout the venue make for a good place to sit and watch the weirdness unfold. It won't be to everyone's taste, but it's a good late-night option after a drink on one of the

terraces along Calle Argumosa.

Olivera, C/ Santo Tomé 8, Chueca
No phone
Open: 9pm–2am (3am Fri/Sat). Closed Sundays.

Pillars and red velvet drapes create an elegant look but lampshades and scattered armchairs make this bar warm and cosy. A soft, yellow glow can

be seen through the front window enticing in passers-by looking for a relaxed drink. Once you've settled into one of Olivera's cush-ioned sofas you won't want to move, except to stumble over to the bar, of course. There's even a piano, but it doesn't often get played. Instead the music is suitably chilled and ambient. The bar is run by Serbs and is named after Yugoslavian movie star Olivera Markovic, whose portrait dominates the room (she looks a little like Catherine Zeta Jones). At

99

weekends, the atmosphere is livelier but you are still guaranteed a chilled experience if you get here early and grab a comfy seat.

Oui, C/ Marqués de Santa Ana 11, Malasaña
No phone
Open: 11pm–3am Thurs, 11pm–3.30am Fri–Sat

Oui is another one of those bars that you probably won't find first time around – but persevere, because it's well worth a look. A frosted glass front lit by fairy lights, along with the inconspicuous looking doorman are all that gives it away, and once inside the originality continues. The venue itself is

one big square-shaped corridor, with the DJ booth tucked away in one corner and the L-shaped bar stretching along two sides of that square. The crowd of regulars are attracted by the dark and atmospheric vibe, and no doubt are friendly with the guys who run it, who have been on the Madrid nightlife scene for longer than they'd care to remember.

El Parnasillo, C/ San Andrés 3, Malasaña
Tel: 91 447 0079
Open: 2.30pm–3am (3.30am Fri–Sat)

Artists, journalists and intellectuals have been gathering here for highbrow conversation for years. Indeed, in the 1970s and 1980s the café was bombed by a far-right group for its part in the cultural revolution. These days, the clientele is still an interesting mix of colourful characters, including the

flamboyant owner, Nina (if she's not busy with her newer venture, Nina, next door (see EAT). The art-nouveau décor, with floral prints, frescos and red velvet banquettes, lends itself well to the overall artsy feel. The bar staff are well trained and will quickly get to know your favourite tipple, whether it's a cocktail or one of Parnasillo's famous alcoholic coffees.

Penthouse, Hotel ME Madrid, Plaza Santa Ana, Centro
Tel: 91 701 60 00 www.memadrid.solmelia.com
Open: 9pm–2am, (3.30am Fri/Sat, 2am Sun). Closed Mon–Weds.

As you wander around the terraces on the newly remodelled Plaza Santa Ana, you may notice a long line of eager punters waiting to enter an eleva-

tor. What awaits them on the top floor is one of the finest outdoor bars in the city: the Penthouse. Part of the M.E. Melia hotel, the Penthouse affords spectacular views of the city, including all of the key landmarks,

such as the Schweppes sign at Callao and the Telefonica clock on Gran Vía. If you know who to talk to up there, you may be able to swing one of the bed-like booth areas, and if you get really lucky you may even end up in the VIP bar, normally reserved for the odd rock star or actor. While the exclusive bar really comes into its own in summer, the crisp, clear evenings of Madrid winter are also enjoyable up on the roof, thanks to several extendable canopies and those now-ubiquitous gas heaters. A soundtrack of soulful house keeps the remarkably mixed crowd entertained, providing great people-watching fare as you ogle everyone from celebs and wealthy tourists, to young Manolete wannabes and ageing rockers.

Puro Placer, C/ Prim 1, Chueca
Tel: 91 521 44 80
Open: 4pm–12.30am (2am Fri) Mon–Fri, 8pm–2am Sat

Despite the best efforts of the EU, there was never any chance that Spaniards were going to part with their nicotine-fuelled ways, and indeed, the so-called smoking ban has been fudged so that you can still light up in

practically any bar, club or restaurant. If you're fond of a puff then, you're going to want to stop by Puro Placer, whose name comes from a play on words thanks to '*puro*' meaning both cigar and pure, and '*placer*' meaning pleasure. The warm orange hues of the décor make for attractive surroundings, clearly visible from the street thanks to the floor-to-ceiling windows. On the menu are wines, whiskies and champagnes, but the real attraction is the specially ventilated humidor, from where you can choose a fat cigar to enjoy, safe in the knowledge that smoking is practically encouraged here.

Ramses, Plaza Independencia 4, Salamanca

Tel: 91 435 16 66 www.ramseslife.com

Open: daily, 8am–3am

Thanks to its Philip Starck-designed interior, and attractive location with views of the Puerta de Alcalá, Ramses has become one of the places to be seen of late, the appeal only heightened by the flashy champagne cocktails that are the speciality from the bar. The door policy is designed to ensure a queue outside at most hours of the evening, and they will turn you away if you're looking even a little scruffy. Once inside, you'll find yourself jostling

for elbow room at the square bar with sugar daddies chatting up much younger girls, handsome Mediterranean types with their squeezes, and groups of glammed-up young ladies looking for someone to buy them a drink. Pass by the restaurant and head down the stairs, and if you're lucky you may be able to blag your way into the basement club, which is usually reserved for private parties but is sometimes open to Joe Public. More a place to see and be seen than one for a rip-roaring good time, Ramses will appeal if you're feeling ostentatious.

Susan Club, C/ Reina 23, Centro

Tel: 91 521 47 79 www.susanclub.com

Open: 9pm–3.30am. Closed Sundays and Mondays.

Popular with young journalistic types, Susan Club is a deceptively large cocktail bar tucked away in the corner of Calle de la Reina, which runs just parallel to the Gran Vía. Order a drink at the top bar as you enter if you want

to enjoy the buzz of conversation in the small space, or head straight downstairs, where you'll find a larger lounge complete with sofas. The all-black interior and very low lighting make for an intimate experience, perfect for a late-night drink if you're already a little worse for wear.

Viva Madrid, C/ Manuel Fernández y Gonzalez 7, Centro
Tel: 91 429 36 40 www.barvivamadrid.com
Open: daily, 1pm–2am (3am Fri–Sat)

One of Madrid's best-known bars, tucked away off the main drag of the Gran Via, it's still heaving most nights. Viva is particularly popular with expats and overseas students, as well as with locals who want to meet them. Everyone is soon tapping their feet to cheesy, commercial tunes that can't

fail to get people dancing. Upstairs tilted mirrors on each wall make the rooms appear bigger and mean that you can check out the talent without being noticed. Be prepared to fight your way to the bar at weekends, but if you're lucky you will have got there early and secured a table out front for a much more civilized experience. If you can't face the crowds, check this place out in the day so you can fully appreciate its tiled décor, romantic prints and vaulted ceiling.

tapas...

While Madrileños love a drink, they rarely get drunk. One of the main reasons for this is, of course, the fact that each drink is often accompanied by a *tapa* – bite-sized snack served with each round.

In cheaper places, tapas will be nothing more than a bowl of olives or a few potato crisps, but head to the right bar, and those tasty morsels will be more appealing than a sit-down meal – and could end up costing you the same, too.

The concept of tapas comes from Andalusia, where a slice of ham or *chorizo* was placed on a small plate that then covered up your glass of wine, thus keeping out dust and flies. The concept then evolved as tavern owners used the custom to ensure customers felt thirstier and therefore bought more drinks.

These days, a whole range of tapas is available in Madrid, from the Basque *pintxo*, which is usually served on a hunk of baguette, to the *tosta*, which is a slice of toast piled high with fresh ingredients such as avocado and tuna, or ham and brie.

Madrid's specialities include *patatas bravas*, chipped potatoes served with a spicy sauce, as well as snails. Galician bars will often serve octopus, prawns and seafood, while many places will even offer little plates of paella.

To order, you'll need to swallow any politeness and reticence, and fight your way to the front of the bar to catch the waiter's attention as soon as possible otherwise you'll be left waiting. Most tapas are on display on the counter, allowing you to point and choose. Waiters have an uncanny knack of remembering what you've had when it comes to ordering the bill, and should they have forgotten, they'll ask you to recap.

In the less upmarket bars, it's not uncommon for diners to throw their napkins and discarded olive pips onto the floor, but before you do that, check out what the locals are doing and follow suit.

Below is a glossary of terms you might find in the tapas bars – most staff don't speak English so it's a very useful crib.

a la brasa – barbecued
a la plancha – grilled
aceitunas – olives
ahumados – smoked fish
ajo – garlic
al ajillo – in a sauce made from olive oil, garlic and chilli
albóndigas – meatballs
almejas – small clams
anguila – eel
arroz – rice
bacalao – salted cod
berberechos – cockles
bocadillo – sandwich in a breadroll
boquerones – anchovies
calamares – squid rings
callos – tripe
caracoles – snails
cecina – smoked or dried meat
chorizo – spicy sausage
churros – dough tubes, like doughnuts
cigalas – king prawns
cocido – Madrileño stew
conejos – rabbit
croquetas – croquette, rissole
empanada – small pie
escabeche de atun – marinated tuna
esparragos – asparagus
fagatells – meatball (including liver) skewered to bread
gambas – prawns
gamo estofado – stewed deer

Ibericos y quesos – selection of cold meats and cheese
jamon – dry cured ham
langostinas – langoustines
lomo – loin
marisco – shellfish
mejillónes – mussels
mollejas – sweetbread
morcilla – blood sausage
navajas – razor shells
ostras – oysters
pan – bread
papas – fried potatoes/chips
parillada – mixed grill
pechinas – scallops
percebes – barnacles
pescaditos – whitebait
pimientos rellenas – stuffed pepper
pincho – kebab
pulpo – octopus
puntillitas – tiny squid
salazones – salted fish
salchicha – sausage
salpicon de marisco – mixed shellfish
sepia – cuttlefish
tinto – red wine
tosta de cabrales – toasted bread and cheese

4 de Tapas, C/ Barbieri 4, Chueca
Tel: 91 523 94 64 www.4detapas.com
Open: 9am–5pm, 7pm–2am Mon–Sat

Located in the heart of Chueca, 4 de Tapas serves a great selection of bite-sized *tostas*, as well as salads and stews, to an eager, cool and smart crowd

of locals. If you don't feel like snacking at the bar, you can grab a seat at the restaurant area at the back, which seats around 40. The beige walls and dark wood of the interior make for a modern and stylish setting, while the clientele are very keen on the long drinks doled out by the young staff come the end of a meal.

Almendro 13, C/Almendro 13, La Latina
Tel: 91 365 42 52
Open: 1–4pm, 7pm–midnight Mon–Fri; 1–5pm, 8pm–1am Sat–Sun

If you're looking for great tapas, then a visit to Almendro 13 is a must – be prepared to have to fight your way in, however, as this traditional wood-panelled bar gets rammed both at weekends and during the week, when many other places would be quieter. Tucked away on the corner of a side street the bar is beloved of the local community who come time and time again. There's a good reason for the crowd, though, namely the classics it serves, such as the *huevos rotos* (fried eggs and potatoes), the *roscas rellenas* (bread stuffed with meat) and, breaking the *tinto* stranglehold, its very own *manzanilla* sherry. There are two different counters, one for ordering food and one for ordering drinks, so be on the lookout for your snack as it

appears out of the kitchen hatch – although a little bell does ring to catch your attention.

La Bardemcilla, C/ Augusto Figueroa 47, Chueca

Tel: 91 521 42 56 www.labardemcilla.com
Open: 1–4pm, 8.30pm–1am. Closed Saturday lunch and Sundays.

The name may sound a little familiar, the reason being that this quaint tapas bar is run by the sister of Oscar-winning actor, Javier Bardem. But rather

than relying on that famous surname to get punters through the door, Mónica has created a place that turns our excellent versions of the staple options, such as pota-to croquettes, meat-balls and chorizo. If there aren't celebrities dining there on your visit, then you can enjoy perusing the Bardem family album plastered onto the walls – after all, Ma Bardem was also an actress, and there are several other famous members of the clan out there asw well. A small gripe would be the service, which can be, frankly, poor. But get there just before the 3pm rush, and you should get served quickly enough.

La Carpanta, C/ Almendro 22, La Latina
Tel: 91 366 57 83
Open: daily, 1pm–1am

This stylish tapas bar/restaurant is always bursting with people who come here for the lively, friendly atmosphere, its selection of over 50 wines, the fabulous food and a chance to gawp at the rather stunning-looking staff. La

Carpanta is run by a family of Madrileño actors who have tastefully furnished it with quirky wooden furniture and flowery window boxes. Apart from that, it's just bare brick walls and wooden floors. If you want to secure one of the tables in the back rooms, add your name to the waiting list and join the throngs in the front bar. Thursday to Saturday you might have to wait up to an hour, but it's worth it (especially for the meatballs).

Casa Labra, C/ Tetuán 12, Centro
Tel: 91 531 00 81 www.casalabra.es
Open: daily, 9.30am–3.30pm, 5.30–11pm

Just off Sol, in the middle of Madrid's hectic 'high-street' shopping district,

sits this legendary bar. The birthplace of the Spanish Socialist Party in 1879, Casa Labra has lots of charm – if you're prepared to overlook the slow, po-faced waiting staff (who look ready for retirement and seem to begrudge your every request) and the rather drab look of the place. As well as its historical significance, it's known for its *bacalao* (cod in fried batter) and *croquetas* (creamy croquette potatoes), which are served from the small, original zinc counter in the front room. You may have to queue a while before they take your order, but once you've got your drink and tapa you can head out on to the street to enjoy them with the rest of the clientele.

Los Gatos, C/ Jesús 2, Centro

Tel: 91 429 30 67
Open: noon–1am (2am Fri–Sat). Closed Sundays.

There's paraphernalia everywhere in this fun, down-to-earth tapas joint. You

name it, it's either hanging on the walls or plonked in a corner. The more bizarre objects of decoration include a rather garish statue of a choirboy wearing sunglasses, an old motorbike, several glass-encased football shirts, a street lamp and a bull's head. The atmosphere is casual and lively, bordering on raucous in the evenings. Goodness knows what they put in the beer but everyone in here has a smile on their face. A tiny counter, crammed in among all the odd objects, displays the delights on offer. Behind this, staff pour *cañas* by the dozen as the orders are shouted across. It's cheap, definitely cheerful and well worth a visit.

Juana la Loca, Plaza Puerta de Moros 4, La Latina
Tel: 91 364 05 25
Open: 8pm–2.30am (12.30am Mon) Mon–Fri; 1pm–2am Sat–Sun

The chef behind this L-shaped bar takes his tapas very seriously, even providing diners with a knife and fork to attack them, rather than leaving them

to use their hands. An extensive menu is available, complete with larger dishes such as *hummus* and the delicious oxtail. But the best way to decide what to have is to check out the huge doorstop

tapas at the bar, and point out to your waiter the ones you fancy. The low lighting and small number of covers makes for a cosy experience, apart from at peak times such as weekend nights and Sunday afternoons, when it's standing room only. Perhaps the one blight is the newly installed plasma screen TV that is mounted on the wall, but assuming your conversation is stimulating enough, that and the excellent food will ensure your attention doesn't wander to the idiot box.

Lamiak, C/ Cava Baja 42, La Latina

Tel: 91 365 52 12   www.lamiak.net
Open: 12.30pm–1am. Closed Mondays.

Like many a bar in La Latina, Lamiak really comes into its own on a Sunday, when a DJ takes to the decks in the corner to provide a soundtrack for the

constant stream of afternoon drinkers who float in and out of the packed venue. This is a Basque-style place, with huge *pintxos* piled with all sorts of delicious ingredients sat atop the counter, just waiting for you to pick them. If you don't fancy the usual beer or long drink, you can also plump for an Asturian cider. The crowd is young and friendly, as reflected by the various outlandish exhibitions of artwork and photography that often adorn the walls. It's not a place for a quiet drink, but it is a chance to see the neighbourhood at its best.

Lateral, C/ Fuencarral 43, Chueca

Tel: 91 531 68 77   www.cadenalateral.es
Open: daily, 10am–midnight

The team behind Lateral, who have actually opened four branches of this restaurant, have hit on a winning formula, taking traditional tapas recipes and serving them in minimalist surroundings. The fact that this branch, the first one to open, is right next to that epicentre of cool, the Mercado de Fuencarral shopping mall, won't have done them any harm at all. But that's not to say that the venture isn't worthy of the success it has garnered. Lateral attracts a young and frighteningly good-looking crowd, who range

from the smartly turned out to the fittingly grungy. The range of different shades of vodka behind the bar will be enough to tempt you into having a long drink to accompany your tapas, but there's a decent selection of wines, too, if that's what you fancy.

Mercado de la Reina, C/ Gran Vía 12, Centro
Tel: 91 521 31 98 www.mercadodelareina.es
Open: daily, 9am (10am Sat/Sun)–midnight (1am Sat)

As time passes, the centre of Madrid is gradually seeing the invasion of the usual globalization culprits. Hats off then to the team behind Mercado de la Reina, who have managed to install a top-notch tapas joint, restaurant and gin bar smack bang on Gran Vía – a street that's home to everyone from Burger King and McDonalds, to H&M and Nike. Crates of fresh vegetables adorn the walls, a nod to the quality produce behind the dishes on offer,

while there are even trees installed inside, housed in giant plant pots. Smart, suited Spaniards pack the place out on weeknights, while a cooler crowd drops by come the weekend. Be sure not to leave before venturing right to the back of the deep venue, where you'll find the Gin Club (open from 4pm every day) for some Hogarthian supping.

Stop Madrid, C/ Hortaleza 11, Chueca

Tel: 91 521 88 87   www.stopmadrid.es
Open: daily, noon–2am

Founded way back in 1929, Stop Madrid manages to be at once a traditional tapas bar but also a magnet for a cool, Chueca crowd. Located on the corner of Calle Fuencarral, just around the corner from Gran Vía, the bar itself will get your mouth watering as soon as you set eyes on it. Glistening hams hang alongside spicy sausages and *morcillas* (a fantastic kind of blood sausage/black pudding, should you have the stomach for that sort of thing), while open plates of all kinds of tuna and seafood sit underneath the glass counter. The great selection of wines provides a perfect accompaniment to the tapas and *raciones* on offer, and while the service may not be the friendliest, it is at least efficient.

Taberna del Alabardero, C/ Felipe V 6, Centro

Tel: 91 547 25 77
Open: daily, 1–4pm, 9pm–midnight

Located just behind the Teatro Real, this is a quintessentially Spanish tapas bar and restaurant. Simple café rooms at the front have marble tables and deep red banquettes, while at the back red and white tablecloths and elegant place settings play host to locals and tourists alike.

The selection of tapas is a cut above what is normally on offer, but this – and its prime location – are certainly reflected somewhat in the price. The staff are charming and have a vague smattering of English to help you understand what you are actually going to order. This is tapas at its best.

Taberna Maceira, C/ Jesús 7, Centro
Tel: 91 429 15 84
Open: 1pm–4.30pm, 8.30pm–1am (1.30am Friday–Saturday)

This funky Galician tapas bar is like none other in Madrid. Its walls are painted in splodges of green (almost like the work of a class of schoolchildren), but the result gives

the interior a vibrant twist. Even the menus are a novelty, scrawled on round wooden artists' palettes. The cheery décor creates a relaxed mood and attracts Madrid's bohemian, arty set, who chatter away while traditional Galician bagpipe music plays in the background. The speciality is octopus and everyone seems to be eating it, along with other favourites such as salted roasted peppers (totally addictive) and *patatas bravas*. Staff are casually dressed and work like mad to keep the food and drink coming. Don't miss this place, or its even bigger branch located at C/ Huertas 66.

El Tempranillo, C/ Cava Baja 38, La Latina
Tel: 91 364 15 32
Open: daily, 1–3.45pm, 8pm–midnight

A favourite of in-the-know locals as well as the odd celeb (Real Madrid's Guti is a regular), this exceptional tapas bar has a deservedly fine reputation. The bar boasts a huge wine rack, which is stocked with an ample selection of home grown wines, which are expertly poured by a professional wait staff. The almost rustic interior feels very Spanish indeed, as does the hubbub of animated con-

versation that's ever present. The tapas menu is extensive, with a long list of different types to try, while there are also more substantial dishes on offer if you don't just want to snack. Just be sure to keep an eye out for the reactions of the locals' faces as people walk in – a murmur of excitement will no doubt mean the arrival of a local TV or film star.

La Trucha, C/ Manuel Fernández y González 3, Centro
Tel: 91 429 58 33
Open: daily, 12.30–4pm, 8pm–2am

For authentic Andalusian tapas, try this well-known rustic restaurant, right next door to Viva Madrid (see DRINK). Plates of all shapes and sizes hang

from its whitewashed walls, alongside bunches of garlic and onions, while outside there's a tiny pavement terrace, usually reserved for people eating full meals rather than tapas. The name refers to the fresh trout, which is the speciality of the house, but that doesn't mean you shouldn't try the *pescaito frito* (fried fish) or *berenjena frito* (fried aubergines). Waiters are of the more mature kind and there seem to be dozens of them, all intent on providing top service to the mix of tourists and wealthy (sometimes celebrity) locals who come here.

Txakoli, C/ Cava Baja 26, La Latina
Tel: 91 366 48 77
Open: daily, 8pm (noon Sat/Sun)–2am

Even if you only pop by for a drink, there's no way you'll leave Txakoli without having sampled at least a few of the mouth-watering tapas piled high on the bar. Indeed, the place is always bustling, creating a buzzing atmosphere as the punters enjoy a glass of wine, a *caña* and as many tapas as they can put away. As you order your drinks, simply point at the bite-sized treats that take your fancy, which are topped with anything from quail's eggs and Spanish chorizo, to crab meat and, of course, *jamón*. The service comes

without a smile, as is so often the case in Madrid, unfortunately, but that's the only downside to this great bar.

snack...

While Madrileños have many vices, coffee is perhaps their greatest. Drunk at a times of the day, the seductive liquid is churned out non-stop in all kinds of cafeterías, from the upscale to the traditional. Coffee in Madrid is accompanied by one thing: noise. Just in case the caffeine hit isn't enough to wake you up in the morning, the expert waiters who dish out cup after cup will do so with a cacophony of sound, as beans are ground with a mechanical whirr, cups and spoons are dumped on the counter with a clang, and milk is steamed with a deafening hiss. Then comes a moment of silence, as the inky black espresso is placed before you and the frothy milk added. There are few better ways to begin a day in Madrid.

In the morning, order a *café con leche*, which contains a huge shot of espresso and scalding hot full-fat milk. After dinner, a *cortado* is best, an espresso with ju a splash of milk, while a *café solo* – pure espresso – is good for a pick-me-up a any time.

Cafés buzz throughout the day as groups of workers, friends and solitary patrons come and go, eager to break up their daily grind with plenty of visits t these temples to caffeine. While the inevitable arrival of Starbucks in the capita

ovides a familiar alternative, resist the temptation to enjoy the same skinny tte you could get anywhere in the world, and check out what Madrid has to fer instead.

r a grand experience, head to the Círculo de Bellas Artes, where you can joy the surroundings of Madrid's biggest cultural centre, or for some minimal- environs, order a coffee and a slice of cake at Isolée (below), located on the ge of the fashionable Cheuca district. Here you can buy a magazine, CD or en a Segway once the foam has faded on your cappuccino. Just up the street another achingly hip café, Diurno, which also doubles as a deli, DVD rental re and general meeting point in Chueca.

ome the summertime, head to El Viajero, which boasts a stunning rooftop ter- ce from where you can watch the La Latina neighbourhood go by, while tching a few rays. And for a real Madrid classic, a visit to Café Gijón is a must, meeting point for writers and intellectuals for more than a hundred years.

s not all about coffee though – there are also *churros* to enjoy. Fried rings of tter, *churros* are to be dipped into impossibly thick hot chocolate, either for eakfast or for a very late-night snack. Alternatively grab a *porra*, a long, thick ck of batter that goes better with coffee than chocolate. The only place to mple these when visiting the city is the Chocolatería San Gines, a legendary nue that stays open later than some nightclubs.

Anticafé, C/ Unión 2, The Old City

Tel: 91 559 41 63
Open: daily, 6pm–2.30am

'Are you really anti-coffee or do you serve it here?' That's a question that

husband and wife team Silvia and Manu say they've heard plenty of times since they opened this cute little café, located on the corner of one of the windy streets of Los Austrias. Set on two different levels, the café also doubles as a showroom for Silvia's fashion designs and, fittingly, attracts all kinds of artsy types, from musicians and DJs to budding film directors. As well as the aforementioned coffee, you can enjoy cocktails such as mojitos, long drinks and fruit daiquiris. A new addition to the bar is the pool table now located in the basement, although really this is a place that's better for chilling out than any kind of competitive activity.

Cacao Sampaka, C/ Orellana 4, Chueca

Tel: 91 319 58 40   www.cacaosampaka.com
Open: daily, 10am–9pm. Kitchen open 10am–4.30pm Mon–Fri.

True chocaholics will simply not be able to walk past Cacao Sampaka without popping their head round the door of this shrine to all things crumbly and meltable. But even when you've finished perusing the beautifully presented selection of chocolates on display in the shop, the best is still to come. The adjoining café continues the cocoa-obsessed feel, serving coffees, teas and treats such as jam and chocolate toasties, indulgent pastries and all kinds of hot chocolate drinks. Should you have the sugar shakes by now, you can pick from a menu of salads, sandwiches and soups or even enjoy a beer or a glass of *cava*. Given its location near Alonso Martínez, the clientele is

made up of a mix of nationalities, as evinced by the wide selection of international papers and magazines available to peruse.

Café Acuarela, C/ Gravina 10, Chueca
Tel: 91 522 21 43
Open: daily, 1pm–3am

Even if you didn't know you were in the gay quarter of Chueca, a quick look around your surroundings in Acuarela would be enough to give it away. Customers here are watched over by a benevolent looking angel perched in the large semi-circular window, whose impressive wings are matched by an equally impressive package. The rest of the decoration is equally kitsch, with weathered furniture and ancient photos adorning the walls. A mature crowd comes here to enjoy a tipple or a tea, as the hectic day-to-day life of Chueca plays itself out on the street. The service can be a little snippy –

especially if you dare to request a seat on the 'reserved' sofa — and the soundtrack of tinny house can be annoying, but it's still a Chueca classic, and a great place to warm up an evening.

Café Comercial, Glorieta de Bilbao 7, Malasaña
Tel: 91 521 56 55
Open: daily, 8am–1am (2am Fri–Sat)

One of Madrid's most popular meeting-places, Café Comercial seems to be buzzing at all times of the day and night. In the summer, the prime seats are on the outside terrace where you can watch the world and his *señora* go by. Inside, there's a vast space full of tables. At one time, this would have been an

elegant spot, but today this traditional café has lost much of its splendour. However, this hasn't stopped it drawing in the crowds. Although little has changed in other respects, the owners have brought the café some way into the 21st century by adding internet connections upstairs.

Café de los Austrias, Plaza de Ramales 1, Centro
Tel: 91 559 84 36   www.cafedelosaustrias.com
Open: daily, 9am–midnight (12.30am Fri/Sat)

Located just a short walk from the Teatro Real and the royal palace, Café de los Austrias is a charming place to grab a quick coffee or a glass of wine. The old fashioned interior is presided over by a team of highly attentive wait staff, while a soundtrack of classical music plays out under a buzz of conversation from the older clientele. There's the odd nod to modernity, such as a plasma screen on one wall and the waitresses' PDAs, but this is a

traditional Spanish café through and through. While a full menu is on offer, Café de los Austrias is more suited to an afternoon or early-evening snack, thanks to a selection of 48 teas and 32 hot chocolates. The large undercover terrace outside makes this a real treat come the summer months.

Café de Oriente, Plaza de Oriente 2, Centro
Tel: 91 541 39 74
Open: daily, 8.30am–1.30am (2.30am Fri–Sat)

Since it's right opposite the Palacio Real, in the pretty, leafy pedestrianised Plaza de Oriente, you'd expect to find only tourists here, but this spot is so good the locals love it too. The elegant, traditional terrace café stands on

the site of a former monastery. Waiters are of the more mature kind and, despite being a bit sour-faced, you can tell they know their stuff. Even when every table is taken on the outside terrace (and there are plenty of them), the waiters manage to keep on top of things. Inside, the fake *belle époque* décor, with mirrors, marble table tops and candles, makes Café de Oriente a cosy spot even in the chillier months.

Café del Real, Plaza de Isabel II 2, Centro
Tel: 91 547 21 24
Open: 9am–1am Mon–Thurs; 10am–3.30am Fri/Sat; 10am–midnight Sun

Right on the Plaza de Isabel II, home of Metro Ópera, the Café del Real attracts a steady stream of customers. This cute, unpretentious little place also has a pizzeria downstairs, but don't bother eating here because, to be honest, you'll find better pizzas elsewhere. Instead, stay upstairs in the cosy little café/bar area, or nab a table on the tiny terrace outside (you'll

have to go downstairs to get to it) and enjoy a tasty breakfast, lunch or snack. The Teatro Real is right across the square, so if you're going to watch a performance pop in here  afterwards for a coffee or something stronger.

Café Gijón, Paseo de Recoletos 21, Chueca
Tel: 91 521 54 25   www.cafegijon.com
Open: daily, 7.30am–1.30am (2am Fri–Sat)

Founded in 1888, Café Gijón is perhaps one of the most celebrated meeting points for artists and intellectuals that Madrid boasts. Indeed, the famous name appears everywhere you look inside, whether it's etched onto the

glasses or incorporated into one of the many paintings that adorn the walls. Elsewhere, plaques attest to the long history of the café, such as the one by the door dedicated to "Alfonso, the match seller and anarchist", where Alfonso himself used to ply his wares. Career waiters, grey haired and sporting a white uniform with epaulettes that wouldn't look out of place on a rear admiral, attend to your every whim with efficiency and bonhomie, allowing you to sit back, enjoy your drink and snack and eavesdrop on animated debates between the ageing artsy types who make up the clientele.

Café Vergara, C/ Vergara 1, Centro
Tel: 91 559 11 72
Open: daily, 7.30am–midnight (2am Fri–Sun)

An opulent, traditional café right in the heart of theatreland, Vergara is popular with the artsy crowd. Its cushioned banquettes, gold-painted chandeliers, gilded cherubs and pretty framed portraits all add to its charm and reference the many theatres that stand nearby. The local clientele tend to come here for breakfast *croissants* and lunchtime *tortillas*, but mainly for the delicious cheesecakes and pastries in the afternoon. Due to its location Vergara will always be popular with the guidebook-clutching tourists in pac-a-macs and comfortable shoes – more's the pity. Smartly dressed staff stand ready for action and will do their best to please.

Chocolatería San Ginés, Pasadizo de San Ginés 5, Centro
Tel: 91 365 65 46
Open: daily 9.30am–7am

In Britain, late-night revellers finish the night with a kebab. In Spain, such habits are a little more civilized. Pop by Chocolatería San Ginés in the early hours of the morning, and you'll find a heady mix of wide-eyed clubbers,

tourists fighting to stay awake, and Spanish families, complete with children who should have been in bed hours ago running amok among the tables. Order *chocolate con churros* from the counter as you go in, and then find a seat in the basement to await your cup of treacle-thick hot chocolate and freshly made *churros* – deep fried loops of batter. The street-side terrace makes it a nice option for the daytime, but this is a place best enjoyed after dark.

Circulo de Bellas Artes, C/ Marqués De Casa, Riera 2, Centro
Tel: 91 521 69 42
Open: daily, 9am–1am (3am Fri–Sat)

If you want to enjoy a beer or a coffee in style, then pop into the Círculo

de Bellas Artes, a privately funded cultural centre located in a magnificent building on Calle Alcalá. You'll have to pay €1 to access the centre itself, but it's a small price to pay for the chance to enjoy the view from the huge windows of the bustling city outside. Inside, there are frescos on the ceiling, enormous chandeliers, ornate pillars and an outsized naked statue by Fernando Botero. A varied but cultured crowd tend to frequent the Círculo, all enjoying a chat, a smoke or a quiet read of the papers as a small army of expert waiters deliver beers, wines and of course, coffees. If you can brave the traffic fumes outside, a seat on the terrace is not to be missed.

Delic, Costanilla de San Andrés 14, La Latina
Tel: 91 364 54 50 www.deliccafe.com
Open: daily, 11am (8pm Mon)–2am

If any one venue encapsulates the vibe in the La Latina district, it's Delic, a café and bar that is so oversubscribed on Sunday afternoons that they regularly have to employ a one-in, one-out policy. Among the attractions are the caipahrinas and mojitos, which are churned out by diligent wait staff at a stunning velocity, as well as the home-made cakes, sandwiches, salads and tapas – all of which can also be enjoyed on the outdoor terrace come the summertime. But the real draw is the diversity of the patrons, with glassy-

eyed clubbers still out from the night before and floppy-haired *pijos* all making friends thanks to the fact that its wall to wall in there. Some say it's a bit too popular these days, but Delic is still an essential stop on a Sunday afternoon in La Latina.

Diurno, C/ San Marcos 37, Chueca
Tel: 91 522 00 09 www.diurno.com
Open: daily, 10am (11am Sat/Sun)–midnight (Fri/Sat 1am)

Wander past the window at Diurno and you'd be forgiven for thinking you'd

stumbled on an Apple showroom, as this is where a young and upwardly mobile crowd come to hang out and enjoy the free Wi-Fi with a cup of coffee or a fruit juice. Located in the gay quarter of Chueca, the venue attracts a mixed bunch, who can pick up anything from a salad and a sandwich, to a rental DVD or a tub of Ben & Jerry's. The aforementioned windows also serve as a great spot from which to people-watch, given that the place is situated on one of the area's busier thoroughfares. It's also a worth picking up flyers and free guides to what's on in the city, much of it available in English.

Isolée, C/ Infantas 19, Chueca

Tel: 91 523 98 57 www.isolee.com
Open: 11am–9pm. Closed Sundays.

There are two surprising things about Isolée. First, that such a wide range of cutting-edge elements could exist under one roof; and second, that the space under that roof could be so moderate and still pack it all in. Billed as

a *multiespacios*, Isolée is at once a café, delicatessen, champagne bar, CD shop, Segway dealer, perfumery and newsagents. It's as if it were a one-stop super-shop for the cool-hunter.

The café serves sushi, bagels and fresh juices, while the deli stocks Italian pastas, Mediterranean wines, coffees and teas from around the world and chocolate fondues. You can buy kitchen gadgets or glassware from Carlo Moretti, and give fragrances from Ex Voto a test-squirt. The magazines on offer include Monocle, and you can even buy furniture and accessories from Jonathon Adler. The champagne bar, which stocks Moët and goes by the playful name of the Bubble Lounge, is a must as you venture into Chueca for a night's debauchery. The more pure-minded can enjoy one of the nine brands of mineral water on the menu.

El Viajero, Plaza de la Cebada 11, La Latina

Tel: 91 366 90 64
Open: 1pm–1.30am Tues–Fri 12.30pm–2.30am Sat–Sun

Spread over three stories, this place is everything in one — a restaurant, bar, lounge, pavement café and a garden roof terrace. Found on a corner a minute's walk from Metro La Latina, it's a natural meeting-place for the start of a night's bar-hopping. The ground floor restaurant is a little shabby-looking and serves mediocre food, but the huge first-floor bar/lounge area is a great place to settle into a chair and wait for friends to arrive. A few cocktails later and you'll have probably decided to stay here until closing-time, especially if you've secured one of the more comfortable sofas. In the summer, the best spot is the roof terrace, for a buzzy atmosphere and fabulous views of San Francisco El Grande.

Viva la Vida, Costanilla San Andres 16, La Latina
Tel: 91 366 33 49
Open: 11am–midnight (1am Fri/Sat)

The perfect place to perform a mini-detox after a massive Madrid night out. Juices and smoothies, coffees and teas (and fresh made delicious cakes – okay, so no detox there) are the order of the day. For lunchtimes, though, there is a truly amazing self-service buffet of hot and cold vegetarian food – sold by weight – which features all manner of different veggie takes on the usually highly carnivorous tapas you encounter everywhere else. Viva la Vida also has an excellent wholefood and health food outlet and stocks a wide range of energizing produce to take home or devour on the hoof. Décor is eclectic, bright and infectiously cheery, the Costanilla san Andres branch featuring a fabulous 'Age of Aquarius' fresco in glorious (hippy) technicolour and mosaics of broken mirrors.

party...

When visiting Madrid, remember one thing: sleep is for wimps. It's certainly not for Madrileños. If you're planning on partying in Madrid, you need to make sure you're ready for it. Start drinking at 6pm and you'll be home before most locals have even left the house. You need to pace the night carefully, and make staggering home at 6am your ultimate goal.

Bars will start to fill up around 11pm, as the post-dinner crowd spills out, while pre-club bars, such as Demode, will get busy around 1am. The clubs themselves stay woefully empty until around 2.30–3am, when a queue will suddenly appear at the door and those in the know will start to swan in on the guest lists.

Thursdays are a popular night to go out in Madrid, with the clubs slightly emptier, less bustly and with a more up-for-it and in-the-know crowd. The same can be said of Sunday nights, when the waiters and bar staff of the city enjoy a night out at Weekend safe in the knowledge that they don't have to work come Monday.

Drinks prices have skyrocketed in recent years, with a beer in a nightclub costing around €5 and a long drink around €8 or 9. That said, the measures are huge,

often coming up to fill around half the glass, meaning that you'll have to wait for the ice to melt a little before you can even think about getting it down.

Most clubs include a first drink in their entrance fee, so hang on to the ticket you're given at the door. And, as in most cities, the club scene is inevitably linked to the drug scene, although you're very unlikely to be searched for illicit substances on the door.

Door policies can vary from club to club, but there's normally one queue for the guest list and one queue for Joe Public, so make sure you're in the right one. Unlikely as it may seem, the guest list queue is often longer than the regular one.

Should you see that you're going nowhere fast, however, Madrid is compact enough to head to another venue on foot – if you're not sure where to go, ask someone on the street, as Madrileño clubbers are always friendly and willing to help out.

Cooler venues such as Mondo are very undemanding when it comes to dress code, but if you should head to more upmarket nighteries, such as Moma56 or Pacha, you'll need to dress to impress the doorman – and, even more importantly, those who await you on the inside.

Ananda, Estación de Atocha, Avda. Ciudad de Barcelona, Centro

Tel: n/a   www.ananda.es
Open: nightly during summer from 10pm

No self-respecting clubber would be seen indoors come the scorching
Madrid summertime, so should you be visiting from June to August, head to

Ananda for a nightclubbing experience under the stars. A huge terrace, decorated in an opulent Asian style, features great big beds to laze on, distrib-
uted across 2,000 square metres of space. Inside there's a VIP section, as
well as a minimalist all-white bar. The crowd is a little more mature than
your average Madrid nightery, and the list of local celebs that drop by is
long. The soundtrack on the terrace is 'Buddha Bar' chill-out, while inside
the menu is house. A must for warm summer nights in the city.

Café la Palma, C/ la Palma 62, Malasaña

Tel: 91 522 50 31   www.cafelapalma.com
Open: 12.15am–3.30am Thurs–Sat

This cool little nightspot is divided into three different sections, allowing you
a varied night depending on what you're in the mood for. The bar area is
always buzzing with conversation, and gets busy – but not too busy – come
the weekend. In the middle of the venue is a chill-out area, complete with
thick rugs and comfy cushions, where you can enjoy a beverage horizontally.
The main *sala*, meanwhile, is dedicated to live music, with a carefully picked
roster of local acts. The loyal crowd regularly pay to see acts they've never

heard of before; such is the trust in the Café la Palma team. And once the guitars have been packed away, its time for the DJs to take centre stage, taking you through until chucking out time at around 3.30am.

Cool, C/ Isabel la Católica 6, Centro
Tel: 90 249 99 94 www.fsmgroup.es
Open: midnight–6am Thurs–Sat

With a futuristic, spacey design – right from the impressive staircase that gets you into the club to the bathrooms – Cool is one of the most fashionable places to be seen in on the hedonistic Madrid night scene. There's something for everyone with the nights they put on, starting with

Sunflowers on Thursday, which attracts a young and up-for-it crowd, who enjoy the commercial house the DJs spin. Fridays are Stardust, a polysexual night that's famed for its outlandish S&M dancers and performances, which

play out to a soundtrack of tech house with a hard edge. Then on Saturdays comes Royal, an all-out gay night that's not for the faint-hearted. Like most clubs in Madrid, there'll be no one there until about 3am, so best to turn up around 2am to get settled in and avoid the queue.

Demode, C/ Ballesta, 7, Centro
Open: 11pm–3.30am Thurs–Sat

If you like to keep your clubbing underground, then head to Demode – just be ready to brave some of the city's dodgiest dens along your way. The pre-club bar finds its home in what was once a *bar de putas*, or a hooker bar to you and me. Indeed, its neighbours along the sketchy street Calle Ballesta are still very much in the trade, as the garish neon signs and scantily clad temptresses in doorways attest. To get inside, you'll pass through a kind of sonic airlock, to be greeted by a sparsely lit dance-floor and bar area that is always packed come the weekends. Some of the city's best electro DJs ply their vinyl wares here every week, and the crowd – a gay/straight mix, most of whom are enjoying the first of the night before 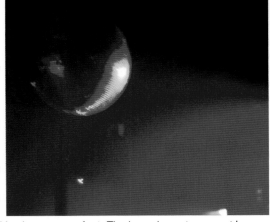 heading on to Mondo – go crazy for it. Thanks to the environment, it's not one for the unadventurous, but it's still a good choice for a bit of harmless vice.

Kapital, C/ Atocha 125, Centro
Tel: 91 420 29 06 www.grupo-kapital.com
Open: midnight–6am Thurs–Sun

The flagship club of the Kapital Group, which runs the biggest nightclubs in the city, Kapital is Madrid's superclub. Set in an old theatre, with a total of seven floors, the venue is a true behemoth on the local scene, catering to a mix of tourists and locals alike. Boasting a main dance-floor, an R&B room, a

cinema and even a merchandise shop, the club offers a host of different musical styles to satisfy every customer. The top floor really comes into its own come the summer, when a retractable roof reveals the night sky. While something of a commercial venue, it's still a failsafe for a good night out – just try not to get lost in there.

Marula, C/ Caños Viejos 3, esq. C/ Bailen 27, The Old City
Tel: 91 366 15 96 www.marulacafe.com
Open: 10pm–5.30am (6am Fri–Sat). Closed Sundays.

If there were an award for cramming the maximum amount of fun into one of the smallest possible places, then it's very likely that Marula would be the hands-down winner. The venue is not much more than the bar area and then a small dance floor, but the funk and soul that are the staple diet of the loyal patrons ensure that such spatial restrictions are not an issue, as every-body gets their groove on. In a marked contrast to the sardine-tin atmos-phere on the inside, the bar boasts a sprawling outdoor terrace come sum-mertime, which, given its location in a little nook underneath the Puente de

Madrid bridge, makes for an attractive spot to enjoy a chilled out *caña* in the cool evening air.

Moma56, C/ José Abascal 56, Chamberí

Tel: 91 399 09 00   www.moma56.com
Open: Weds–Sat 12am–6am

A young, *pijo* crowd comes here for a pose and a bit of a boogie. It's one of those nightclubs that seems bigger than it actually is, thanks to a clever and sometimes confusing arrangement of mirrors. Raised platforms provide a good vantage-point for anyone on the pull (which seems to be most of the

guys and almost as many of the girls). The door policy isn't strict but dress is generally smart and a tiny bit predictable – guys in striped shirts and chinos and girls in black. The commercial house always packs out the dancefloor to a crowd more interested in drink than drugs. The word 'Moma' is emblazoned in red lights wherever you look, in case you forget where you are! Moma is perfect for that 'hang with the kids' glitzy nightclub experience especially if don't mind the cost of the drinks.

Mondo, C/ Arlabán 7, Centro

Tel: 91 523 86 54   www.web-mondo.com
Open: midnight–6am Thurs and Sat

Having started life way back in 1999, Mondo has seen out a refurbishment of its home in Sala Stella as well as a promotion from just a Thursday night affair to a Thursday and Saturday night slot. As a night it has gone from

strength to strength, having first attracted somewhat obscure DJs from mostly European labels, to international heavy hitters such as Josh Wink and A Guy Called Gerald – not bad for a relatively small venue. No one bothers getting there until 3am, so turn up early if you want to have a recce before the punters stream in. The music is all about electro, deep house and techno, which the crowd of friendly regulars goes mental to on the sunken dance-floor.

Pacha, C/ Barceló 11, Chueca

Tel: 91 593 87 69   www.pacha-madrid.com
Open: Weds–Sat 12am–6am

If you've ever visited one of the many Pacha clubs dotted around the globe, you already know what to expect: glamorous, moneyed clubbers there to impress more than to have a great time. Located in an old theatre, the interior of the club is nothing special, although the gorgeous dancers add to the overall ambience of the venue. One thing Pacha does excel in, however, is the effort that goes into their themed nights, with elaborate costumes

and choreographed performances. The music is mostly fairly cheesy house, with plenty of crowd-pleasing mash-ups and the odd crossover hit. Your wallet will take a pounding if you're feeling thirsty, but then that's what a place like Pacha is all about.

Reina Bruja, C/ Jacometrezo 6, Centro
Tel: 91 542 81 93 www.reinabruja.com
Open: 11pm–5.30am Thurs–Sat , 7pm–2am Sun

What used to be a dingy old pool hall run by a few local Chinese has been transformed into one of Madrid's most visually arresting nightclubs. LED lighting, innovative wall designs and a straightfor-

ward layout make for a superb clubbing experience here, particularly on a Sunday evening, when the clubbers who spend all day misbehaving in Space of Sound come to carry on the fiesta. The rest of the weekend sees a smarter crowd, attracted by the commercial tunes churned out by the DJ and the undoubted allure of the interior. If it all gets a bit much for you, head to the chill out area, where you can lounge around on great big red sofas, until you're sufficiently steeled to return to the dance floor.

Shoko, C/ Toledo 86, La Latina
Tel: 91 354 16 81   www.shokomadrid.com
Open: daily, midnight–6am

Fresh from their success in Barcelona, the team behind Shoko have opened this stylish, Asian-themed club in the unlikely location of Calle Toledo. Why

unlikely? Because this working-class end of the city is not the first place you'd expect to find a venue that is so obviously trying to attract a well-heeled crowd. But it is doing well in that respect, pulling in smartly turned-out punters thanks to its *feng shui* interior and adjoining restaurant. The soundtrack from the resident DJs has a suitably cool deep house vibe, although the fact that the venue has yet to be properly soundproofed means that the entire neighbourhood gets to 'enjoy' the tunes. Often used for corporate events and presentations, the club is a bit of a magnet for local VIPs, in particular from the media world, so make sure you know who you're chatting too – it might just be a *famosillo*.

Tempo, C/ Duque de Osuna 8, Centro
Tel: 91 547 75 18 www.tempoclub.net
Open: Café 5pm–3.30am Tues–Fri. Club: 10pm–6am Fri–Sat

It may be a little grimy and somewhat rough around the edges, but Tempo is a great place for a dance if you're not into the glamorous club scene. While

there's a café upstairs for a quieter drink, head down into the basement if you want to enjoy some Gilles Peterson-influenced jazz and funk, from a fine roster of local DJ talent. It's not just your normal long drinks on offer here, thanks to the upstairs café, so be sure to grab a mojito if the fancy takes you. A more mature crowd of media types and music enthusiasts gathers here, ensuring a friendly and welcoming atmosphere.

Weekend, Plaza de Callao 4, Centro
Tel: 91 531 01 32 www.tripfamily.com
Open: noon–6am Sunday

A stalwart of the Madrid scene, Weekend has been the cause of many a Monday-morning hangover, thanks to its excellent soundtrack and well up for it crowd. In fact, they're so up for it, it begs the obvious question – don't these people have jobs to go to? Again, it's a late starter, so don't even bother getting there before about 2.30am. Once there, you'll be treated to an aural feast of Latin house and Brazilian-influenced funk, mostly provided by one of the city's best DJs, Sandro Bianchi. The central location, in a basement in Callao, is just another bonus, because come Monday morning, when the place empties out, you'll want a short walk home.

MUSIC CLUBS

The fact that Madrid is home to the world-renowned flamenco school, Amor de Dios, means that students of the art flock from all around the globe to train here. Flamenco seems to have a global appeal, enjoying popularity in countries as far flung as Japan and Australia. Thanks to the lure of the school, then, the city is one of the best places in the world to see true practitioners of the art. Unfortunately, particularly for the performers involved, the tourist audiences watching are sometimes not aware of the quality musicians and dancers before them, making for a slightly stilted atmosphere at times. The key to watching and enjoying flamenco, then, is to lose any semblance of a stiff upper lip, and let slip the odd 'olé!' as the show reaches its climax.

Most of the flamenco venues mentioned here serve a meal before the show, and although the food can be of a reasonable standard, it's best to skip what can usually be a pricey option in terms of the quality, and cradle instead a glass of wine as the anguished strains of the music reverberate around the room.

As well as flamenco, Madrid boasts plenty of music clubs, with regular jazz jams, open mic nights and *cuentacuentos*, which roughly translates as storytelling. Check out the weekly *Guia del Ocio* guide to find out exactly what's on.

Café de Chinitas, C/ Torija 7, Centro
Tel: 91 547 15 02 www.chinitas.com
Open: 8.30pm–1am Mon–Sat. Shows at 10.30pm and 12.15am.

Featuring what seems like a cast of thousands, complete with castanets and dresses with long trains, the flamenco show here is definitely the more touristy of those on offer in the city. That said, it is visually spectacular, and all set in a very old school environment, thanks to the mature waiters in white shirts and the rustic decoration. The show is long, lasting nearly two hours, so you'll be getting your money's worth – no bad thing considering it is also one of the pricier places to pick.

Las Carboneras, Plaza del Conde de Miranda 1, Centro
Tel: 91 542 86 77
Dinner: 7.30pm and 10pm. Shows: 9pm and 10.30pm Mon–Thurs, 8.30pm and 11pm Fri–Sat. Closed Sundays.

Thanks to a recent renovation, as well as some of the finest flamenco artists appearing regularly, Las Carboneras is considered the best place to see flamenco in the Spanish capital. Each fortnight sees a different guest artist take a turn, usually being the last of the group of dancers to get up and perform. The musicians here are also of the highest calibre – something that can sometimes be wasted on the audience sat at the tables, but greatly appreciated by the locals, who usually congregate at the bar. The maitre d', Kike, will keep you amused, while the rest of the staff speak all kinds of languages. Thanks to the varied clientele it attracts, the restaurant has even had its menu translated into Japanese.

Casa Patas, C/ Cañizares 10, La Latina
Tel: 91 369 04 96 www.casapatas.com
Open: 1–4.30pm, 8pm–midnight Mon–Thurs; 1–4.30pm, 7.30pm–1am Fri–Sat. Shows at 9pm, 10.30pm and midnight.

Unlike at some of the other flamenco clubs, at Casa Patas dinner and dancing are kept separate, meaning you can enjoy your meal before heading through into the other section of the bar to watch the show. The small tables inside give a sense of intimacy, bolstered by the fact that there are usually just two dancers performing. If you want to mingle with the performers and those in the know once the show is over, nip across the street to the sister bar, where you can congratulate the dancers on their *duende*.

Corral de la Morería, C/ de la Morería, The Old City
Tel: 91 365 84 46/11 37 www.corraldelamoreria.com
Open: daily, 8.30pm–2am

Follow in the footsteps of Frank Sinatra and Ava Gardner and enjoy some top flamenco acts at this serious venue. You'll have to pay for such quality, however: the cost of food and drink is particularly steep, but the menu is excellent. Originally opened in 1957, it hosts some excellent shows, transporting the viewer back in time. Although it's touristy, it's not too showy and feels suitable earthy.

La Solea, C/ Cava Baja 27, La Latina
Tel: 91 369 41 43
Open: 8.30pm–3am. Closed Sundays.

For a truly genuine flamenco experience, this is the place. It's like nothing you will have seen before or are likely to see again. Two tiny rooms are packed full of enthusiasts and gradually people start to sing or play guitar. Soon the whole place is wrapped in a swirl of emotion. It can be slightly intimidating at first but, with the help of a few drinks, you'll soon find yourself getting into the flamenco spirit. 'Visitors' are welcome, but you might find there's standing-room only.

JAZZ

Café Central, Plaza del Angel 10, Centro
Tel: 91 369 41 43
Open: noon–1.30am (2.30am Fri–Sat). Closed Sundays.

Once voted one of the world's top jazz venues by *Wire* magazine, this art-deco café is definitely worth a visit if you're into all things jazz. Varied programmes of local and international acts perform in the elegant, high-ceilinged room. Top names, such as George Adams, Don Pullen and Bob Sands, have all graced the stage, alongside lesser-known but equally entertaining Spanish acts. The atmosphere is laid-back and low-key, and you'll be close enough to the stage to get the full jazz effect.

Café Jazz Populart, C/ Huertas 22, Centro
Tel: 91 429 84 07 www.populart.es
Open: daily, 6pm–2.30am (3.30am Fri–Sat). Performances: 11pm & 12.30am.

This narrow bar hosts mostly jazz, but you might also get to see musicians playing blues, soul, Cuban, flamenco and even reggae. It's small, intimate and, centrally located among the bars and restaurants of calle Huertas, it's always busy. We advise getting here early if you want to secure a good spot, close to the performers.

ADULT ENTERTAINMENT

There are two main red-light districts in Madrid. The first is centred around Calle Montera in the city centre and spills over onto the other side of the Gran Vía. It's what you'll find in any other major city, with a plethora of strip joints, sex shops and bored-looking women swinging their handbags. The laws surrounding prostitution in Spain are complicated. It's not illegal to pay for sex, or to solicit it, but it is against the law to pimp. In the past, the prostitutes working in the Calle Montera area have worked for themselves, are known to the police, and have been left to operate with little bother from the authorities. In recent years, however, an increasing number of Madrid's prostitutes are coming from Africa, Latin America and Eastern Europe, and it has become obvious that these groups are largely controlled by mafias. Occasionally there are high-profile raids but largely these rackets carry on unrestricted. The influx from overseas has, however, swelled the industry and the authorities have taken the rather strange decision to move the prostitutes out of the centre and into Madrid's vast park, the Casa de Campo on the western edge of the city.

Along the main access roads that run through the park you'll find scantily clad women and transvestites lurking in the trees, waiting for passing traffic, day and night. If you take the Teleférico cable car across the park you will see them standing around, chatting to kerb crawlers. It doesn't seem to deter the Madrileños from enjoying the park, however, and couples and families carry on with their picnics and afternoon walks undeterred.

Oz Teatro, General Orgáz 17, Madrid
Tel: 91 449 05 86 www.ozmadrid.com
Open: 7pm–4am. Closed Sunday and Monday.

Oz Teatro is a large American-style table-dancing bar where very good-looking women strip on stage or at your table. Housed in an impressive old theatre, close to the Bernabeu football stadium, it is a cut above the back-street peep-shows and dancing clubs. Sophisticated and stylish… well, as much as a strip club can be… the complex houses a restaurant and bar as well as the club itself. In this department, the best that Madrid has to offer.

Hg2 Madrid
culture...

The Prado Museum is perhaps Madrid's most famous cultural landmark, home to some of the finest paintings in Europe. The works of Goya, Velázquez and Caravaggio all grace the walls, while the temporary exhibitions attract visitors from all over Europe. It is a must for all those visiting the city for the first time, and for those returning, thanks to the new wing designed by architect Rafael Moneo, unveiled in 2007.

Close by, but by no means less important, are the Thyssen and the Reina Sofia. The Thyssen is home to the collection of Baron Thyssen-Bornemisza, who put together a remarkable selection of Impressionist and Post-Impressionist art, housed in a beautiful palace, which has been transformed into a contemporary hanging space.

The Reina Sofia houses one of Picasso's most famous works, *Guernica*, as well as some impressive pieces by Miró and many other works by 20th century artists. A recent extension to the building, designed by Jean Nouvel gives it a greater exhibition space, as well as a well-stocked bookshop and popular café.

Adding to this so-called 'golden triangle' of art museums around the Paseo del Prado is the new CaixaForum, an intriguing building that hosts constantly

hanging exhibitions, many drawn from the artistic holdings of savings bank La Caixa, which is behind the new space.

Madrid's cultural life doesn't necessarily revolve around tramping through art galleries, since there are some beautiful parks to explore. The Retiro is more formal than the wilderness landscape of Casa de Campo and on a par with the stunning gardens of the Palacio Real. Madrid's public spaces and architecture are among the most breathtaking of any European city. Try to incorporate the Plaza Mayor and the Palacio Real into your tour of the city.

Madrid might not spring to mind as a leading capital for theatrical entertainment, but nevertheless it holds its own. The mixture of large, major venues and smaller, alternative ones means there is something to suit every taste.

Like the bigger art galleries, many of the theatres are closed on Mondays and most of the alternative venues are only open from Thursday to Sunday. As with everything else in Madrid, performances start late, at around 9–10pm, and at the weekends there are sometimes second, even later showings.

For programmes detailing what's on, get the local guide, *La Guia del Ocio*, or look in the Friday listings in the daily newspapers. *El País*'s OnMadrid supplement is particularly useful.

Tickets range from €12 to €40 and are often cheaper on Mondays, Wednesdays and/or Sundays. They can be bought over the phone through La Caixa Catalunya (90 210 12 12 or www.telentrada.com) and Caja Madrid (90 22 16 22 or www.entradas.com), from El Corte Inglés (90 240 02 22 or www.elcorteingles.es) or directly from the theatres themselves.

In October and November, Madrid plays host to the Festival de Otoño, which attracts big international names from the world of theatre, while February brings the fringe festivals of theatre and dance – Escena Contemporanea and La Alternativa. Madrid's alternative theatre scene is tame in comparison with other cities, but it is flourishing, with venues thriving all around the city.

CaixaForum, Paseo del Prado 36, Centro

Tel.: 91 330 73 00   www.laCaixa.es/ObraSocial

Open: daily, 10am–8pm

An extraordinary piece of construction, from architectural innovators Herzog & de Meuron, the CaixaForum is a sponsored arts foundation from

one of Spain's leading banks. The intriguing building, designed to mirror the roofscape of the surrounding buildings, houses several exhibition floors, which host a constantly changing selection of temporary shows. The cantileverd exterior gives the outward appearance a feeling of ethereal lightness that defies the laws of gravity and sucks aesthetes into the impressive minimally modern internal space. The CaixaForum is as much a piece of art as the works housed inside.

Casa de Campo and the Teleférico, Paseo Pintor Rosales

www.teleferico.com

Teleférico open: noon–8pm in summer, noon–9.30pm in winter

This huge, 4,500-acre woodland on the western side of the River Manzanares is home to the city's zoo, swimming pools, tennis courts, a boating lake, funfair and cafés. Once you stray from the main roads, it becomes pretty wild, with large stretches of woods and gullies. You'll only be able to cover a small part of it by foot, or even by bike, but take the Teleférico cable car from the edge to the middle and you'll get a better idea of the sheer size of this city wilderness. If you look carefully, you'll also spot the semi-clad prostitutes loitering among the trees and bushes. Day and night, female

and transvestite prostitutes parade their wares along the main roads, but don't deter the locals from enjoying their picnics or afternoon strolls.

Centro de Arte Reina Sofía, C/ de Santa Isabel 52, Centro

Tel: 91 774 10 00   www.museoreinasofia.es
Open: daily, 10am–9pm (2.30pm Sun)

This huge exhibition space (formerly a hospital) houses contemporary Spanish art, 20th-century works from the Prado, and the Miró and Picasso legacies, including the famous Guernica. Its white walls, high ceilings and vast galleries are ideal for these modern and often large-scale works. The

museum also has a theatre, cinema, library, restaurant and bar and from its top, fourth floor there are fabulous views across to Atocha station. An extension project, designed by Jean Nouvel and inaugurated in 2005, has added yet more exhibition space, as well as an excellent bookshop and café.

El Rastro, C/ Ribera de Curtidores, La Latina
Open: 8am–2pm Sun

Madrid's main flea market is as much a place to enjoy for its atmosphere and culinary offerings as it is for what you can buy there. By 11am on a

Sunday the sea of visitors swarms through the seemngly endless narrow lanes left by the rows of stalls, which sell everything from incense and t-shirts, to army surplus and flamenco CDs. Be sure to stop by the endless cafés and bars that line the route to enjoy beers, tapas or even a plastic cup filled with olives.

Museo del Prado, Paseo del Prado, Centro.
Tel: 91 330 29 00 www.museodelprado.es
Open: Tues–Sun 9am–8pm

Known simply as the Prado, this museum houses one of the oldest and

most important collections of art in the world. Two centuries of the finest works, collected by Spanish royalty, are shown in this magnificent building. You could easily spend several days here if you wanted to experience it to the full. However, if you've only got an afternoon you must see the works of Spanish artists Goya (especially his Black Paintings), Velázquez and El Greco. Don't bother with a guided tour but do invest in the miniature books on selected artists, sold in little dispensers in the exhibition rooms. A recent extension project from the architect Rafael Moneo, unveiled in 2007, constitutes the biggest change to the museum in its more than 200 years of history, giving the institution more space for complementary activities.

Museo Thyssen Bornemisza, Paseo del Prado 8, Centro.
Tel: 91 369 01 51 www.museothyssen.org
Open: 10am–7pm. Closed Mondays.

More than 1,000 pieces of art, assembled by avid collector Baron Thyssen-Bornemisza, who died in April 2002, are on display in this neo-classical palace, which is now presided over by the late Baron's wife, an ex-Miss Spain. Works span the 14th to the late 20th century and are mainly by European artists, including Degas, Manet, Cézanne, Van Gogh, Matisse, Picasso, Munch and Constable. Due to the relative small scale of the collection visitors are treated to a visual understanding of how art developed out of the dark ages and into the present day; the layout of the galleries allows for immediate comprehension without overwhelming the  senses. Complementary exhibitions are often to be found in the Fundación Caja Madrid building, located in Plaza San Martín, just near Ópera (www.fundacioncajamadrid.es).

Palacio Real, C/ Bailen, Centro

Tel: 91 542 00 59 www.patrimonionacional.es/preal/preal.htm
Open: 10.30am–4.45pm (5.45pm April–Sept) Mon–Sat, 10am (9.30am
April–Sept)–1.30pm Sun

It took 26 years to build the splendid Palacio Real, and King Felipe V, who
commissioned it, was dead long before it was completed. He chose the most
prestigious architects of the day to build it on the site where the Moors
built their original fortress overlooking the Manzanares River. There are

2,800 rooms in all (it was originally going to be four times bigger) but only
50 of them are open to the public. It's probably not worth having the guided
tour, as there's information in each room explaining the key historical and
architectural facts. The highlights are the grand Throne Room and the
Porcelain Room, which is encrusted with 134 Oriental porcelain panels and
silk hangings. Be sure to check out the views of the Casa de Campo from
the central courtyard.

Parque del Buen Retiro

Known as the lungs of a city – and with its pollution levels, Madrid is a city
that really needs good lungs – the Retiro park is one of the focal points of
life in Madrid. Originally part of the palatial grounds of King Felipe IV
(1621–65), the park now attracts every different shade of citizen you could
imagine. Families bring their children here to enjoy the Disney characters on
every corner, young stoners bring their spliffs and bongos to the monument
near the lake to while away the afternoon, and all kinds of fitness freaks get

an aerobic rush from propelling themselves around the park, whether on foot or on wheels. It's also the best place to pick up hash from the many African dealers who are there selling all day long.

Plaza de Cibeles, Centro

As well as being a major traffic junction, the intersection of the Paseo del

Prado and Calle Alcalá are home to one of Madrid's most famous – and most photographed – monuments. The fountain depicts the Greek goddess of nature, Cybele, drawn by two lions, while in the background is the 1904 Palacio de Comunicaciones. This building used to be the central post office in the city, but has since been taken over by the council. Whenever Real Madrid, or indeed Spain, wins a big match, it is here that the fans will head – although the police will be waiting, ready to do anything to keep them from jumping in that famous fountain.

Plaza Mayor

This large, cobbled square was built in 1619 by Juan Gomez de Mora as the town square. Positioned just outside the city walls, it was used by medieval traders to peddle their wares without incurring intra-mural taxation. The ceremonial centre of Madrid, it was used for coronations, markets and bullfights. Today, there  are still plenty of shops in the elegant, arched arcades, some full of tacky souvenirs but others selling fine local crafts. The square's terrace cafés are packed with tourists (there's not a Madrileño in sight), and on Sunday mornings it's transformed into a stamp and coin collector's market. Seasonal markets often also feature, in particular the Christmas one, where you can pick up the funny wigs everyone seems to wear around this time of year, as well as all kinds of figurines for a Bethlehem scene.

Plaza Oriente, Centro.

One of Madrid's most beautiful squares, the Plaza Oriente has manicured gardens, statues, views of the Palacio Real and across the Casa de Campo. It was commissioned by Joseph Bonaparte, Napoleon's brother, and has a very French feel. The equestrian statue of Felipe IV and statues of ancient monarchs were supposed to adorn the royal palace but were thought too heavy. Just down from the park are the Campo del Moro gardens, which in medieval times were used for jousting tournaments. With their winding paths, neat flowerbeds and fountains, the gardens make a lovely, civilized spot for a picnic or to read a book in the sun. The Café de Oriente (see SNACK), nearby, is a great place to enjoy a *café solo* overlooking the gar-

dens, before heading back to the hurly-burly of everyday city life.

THEATRE AND OPERA

Auditorio Nacional de Música, C/ Príncipe de Vergara 146, Centro
Tel: 91 337 01 00   www.auditorionacional.mcu.es

Although not the best-looking venue, this auditorium is hugely popular for its excellent acoustics and comfortable seating. It hosts one of Europe's top classical music festivals and is home to the Orquesta Nacional de Espana.

Teatro Bellas Artes, C/ Marqués de Casa Riera 2, Chueca
Tel: 91 532 44 38   www.teatrobellasartes.es

A stunning old theatre that stages some very good shows. More adventurous productions are shown at the Círculo, housed in the same building.

Teatro Real, Plaza de Isabel II. Centro
Tel: 91 516 06 00   www.teatro-real.es

Reopened after a €120-million and much-delayed renovation, Madrid's main opera and dance venue is finally making its mark. It's believed to be the most technically advanced theatre in Europe, and indeed the acoustics and effects are stunning, making the most of the top opera, ballet and musical performances now being shown here.

Veranos de la Villa
www.esmadrid.com/veranosdelavilla
Festival runs July–mid-September

The likes of B.B. King, Erykah Badu, Caetano Veloso and Macy Gray have graced the stage at the Centro Cultural Conde Duque during the summer months thanks to this partly council-funded festival. July is given over to rock, jazz, blues and Latin music while August brings flamenco and ballet. In the spring, you can enjoy dance performances of all kinds during the city's dance festival, Madrid en Danza. Although the main concert season runs from October to June, there are many open-air performances.

Notes & Updates

shop...

If Madrileños aren't eating or drinking in their spare time, they're invariably partaking in their other favourite pastime – shopping. In Madrid, looking good is paramount as much for men as for women, and wearing the latest fashion and the right designer labels means hitting the shops regularly, even in the hot summer months.

On the whole Madrileños tend to dress pretty conservatively, and it's not uncommon to see mothers and their young daughters, or fathers and sons, wearing similar-style clothes. But that doesn't mean that more funky, alternative fashion is not an option here.

There are several distinct shopping areas in the city, catering to different tastes and bank balances. For example, if you want designer stores and money is no object, head for Salamanca, where the likes of Gucci, Versace and Chanel sit side by side. If you're in search of a bargain, stick to the shopping streets around Sol with its predominance of high street fashion – think Oxford Street not Bond Street. If you want something that is a little different and slightly edgy head to Chueca or TriBall, where the more bohemian and alternative shops are found.

Guide book lore would have it that no shopping trip to Madrid is complete without a visit to its famous Sunday morning market, El Rastro (see page 152), although if you're familiar with London's Portobello or Les Puces at Clignancourt in Paris, you might be disappointed by the comparatively limited selection. Other than this, La Latina shopping is mainly unremarkable.

Shops in the city centre open at around 10am and close as late as 8pm or 9pm Monday to Friday, although some smaller, independently owned shops will shut for three hours at 2pm. On Saturdays doors open slightly later at 10.30am, while most shops open every first Sunday of the month.

If you're short on time but want to treat yourself to some retail therapy, head to El Cortes Inglés. Here, in Spain's only chain of department stores, you'll find high-quality fashion, homeware, accessories and pretty much everything else all under one roof (although sometimes stores are split across streets).

Good value high-street fashion chains Zara and Mango are dotted all over the city and are cheaper than in the UK. There's even a Zara seconds store on Gran Vía where you can pick up bargains.

Sales usually run January–February and July–August. Be aware that if you are paying with a credit card, you will often be asked for photo ID, so carry your passport or driver's licence with you.

Calle Jorge Juan

Barbour the classic English country outfitter is a big hit among the Salamanca yuppie crowd.

Blunauta women's daywear for the urban country set

Brioni the byword in sumptuous, Italian made to measure suits, as sported by the likes of Cary Grant, Clark Gable, Pierce Brosnan and, er, Donald Trump

Christofle beautiful silverware, jewelry and gifts

Etro colourful, slightly bohemian fashion for men and women from the Italian designer

Gant elegant flagship store in a beautiful building

Hackett classic British tailoring

La Martina everything you could possibly want for playing – or more likely watching – a game of polo... Ralph Lauren eat your heart out

Weekend tiny boutique selling the likes of Ralph Lauren

Callejón Jorge Juan

A small cul-de-sac that leads off the larger Calle Jorge Juan, this is the home to elegant Spanish designer shops that pull in the ladies who lunch of Salamanca. Having exhausted your credit card, pop down the road for a long lunch at Matilda.

Boxcalf specializes in leather jackets, accessories made in Mallorca and a line of particularly elegant umbrellas

Cashmere Concept 80% of the stock on the shelves here is made from cashmere, with labels such as Rivamonti, Ballantynes and Brunello Cucinelli, known as the king of cashmere. Come summer it's all about cotton and silk, with everything on offer made of natural materials.

Scooter catering to men and women, carries mostly French brands, in particular Vanessa Bruno and Antik Batik. Look out for the selection of unique accessories, for which the owner has scoured the globe.

Sybilla one of Japan's most favoured designers, Sybilla has branched out from her own name brand, which specializes in simple, stylish clothes, with

offshoot Jocomomola (which roughly translates as "wow, that's really cool").
Check out her original Madrid showroom here in Jorge Juan.

Calle Jose Ortega Y Gasset

Cabranes Joyero long established watch and jewelry store. Very classic in
taste, but worth a visit.

Calvin Klein CK superstore on three levels

Chanel classic elegance from the legendary Parisian design house

Elena Benarroch leading Spanish shoe and leatherware designer

Escada fabulous womenswear, accessories and perfumes

Giorgio Armani flagship for the couture label

Hermes for the fashionista with equestrian tendencies

Kenzo elegant and colourful fashions

Lavinia amazing range of wines and highly knowledgable staff, with tastings
held and a café bar and restaurant upstairs

Louis Vuitton the byword in elegant travel goods and accessories

Calle Serrano

Madrid's smartest shopping street and home to all the top designer names,
Calle Serrano is always heaving with traffic and shoppers. Its up-market, air-
conditioned shopping mall, Galería ABC Serrano, is a good spot for browsing on a hot day and boasts a fine selection of boutiques including some
high fashion names. The well-known department store El Corte Inglés also
has branches at numbers 47 and 52, although they are not as large as the
stores on Calle Goya. More interesting boutiques are to be found on the
streets surrounding Serrano, particularly Lagasca, Jorge Juan and Claudio
Coello.

Adolfo Dominguez the best of many Madrid outlets from Spain's leading
fashion designer

Armani Collezioni one of three Armani presences in Madrid. Giorgio
Armani is at C/ José Ortega Y Gasset 16, while Emporio Armani is at C/
Juan Bravo, 1.

Bimba & Lola great Spanish brand, offering wearable, graceful women's
fashion with an emphasis on indulgence and fun

Carolina Herrera flagship store of the New York based, Venezuelan born designer

Cartier a little further up the street from the pack is Cartier's main Madrid store

Diesel also in Chueca on C/ Fuencarral

Ermenegilda Zegna sensationally chic menswear from the Italian designer who is perhaps undeservedly less well known than Armani

Farrutx women's fashion and accessories, but it's the shoes that absolutely shine in this Salamanca must see

Geltra reasonably priced leatherwear, shoes and accessories

Hoss smart and trendy womenswear, also on C/ Fuencarral

La Perla Italian lingerie and swimwear label

Loewe founded in 1872, Loewe is the byword in classic Spanish leather accessories

Longchamp cool, understated French luggage and accessories

Musgo an eclectic mish mash of very stylish homeware, gifts, fashion and accessories for adults and children. Great window displays.

Pedro del Hierro slick, cosmopolitan and elegant womenswear from a Spanish label with a sadly only limited presence outside of Spain

Purificacion Garcia elegant and discreet daywear from another interesting Spanish designer

Tommy Hilfiger king of the classic American preppy

Yves Saint Laurent flagship store for the French design legend

Elsewhere in Salamanca

Antonio Pernas, C/ Claudio Coello 46 another noteworthy local designer who is making an impact internationally

Beverley Hills Polo Club, C/ Goya 6 polo shirts, country classic clothing and accessories

DKNY, C/ Velázquez 28 Donna Karan's more affordable line appeals to a younger set

Ekseption, C/ Velázquez 28 huge range of fashion and accessories from a host of well-known international top end designers

Espacio Chus Burés, C/ Claudio Coello 88 bold and unsual jewellery and accessories from another one of Spain's leading designers

Lotusse, C/ Goya 6 shoe and leather accessories specialist, stocking own brand and the likes of Sebago and Timberland

Prada, C/ Goya 4 just 2 paces off C/ Serrano is the Prada flagship store in Madrid

CENTRO

Calle Preciados and Calle Carmen

Just off Puerta del Sol, these two pedestrianized streets are dedicated to high-street names and smaller one-off shops selling cheap and moderately priced clothes, shoes and accessories. There are three large branches of El Corte Inglés here and a large branch of Zara (although there is an even bigger one a short walk away in the Gran Vía). Weave your way in and out of groups of teenage girls and tourists, and the occasional busker, and hunt out the bargains. Watch out for pickpockets, however, who regularly operate in this area.

Area Real Madrid, C/ Carmen 3 one of the most famous football clubs in the world became something of a vehicle for selling t-shirts during the era of the *galácticos*. They may be long gone, but the clothing machine continues to function, here at their central store.

Casa Jiménez, C/ Preciados 42 founded in 1923, this impressive traditional shop specializes in *mantonas* (Spanish shawls), *mantillas* (silk headscarves) and fans.

El Cortes Inglés, C/ Preciados 1–4 whatver you're looking for, you'll find it in El Corte Inglés. There are three different shops around Preciados, each specializing in different sections, such as electrical, clothing and groceries.

FNAC, C/ Preciados 28 rather like a Spanish Foyles (London's leading independent bookstore), FNAC has an amazing book catalogue, a reading room and is spread over three floors

Sun Planet, C/ Preciados 33 one of many branches of the Spanish sunglasses chain

Zara, C/ Preciados 14 one of the many branches of this Spanish store to be found in the capital, which has been exported to all corners of the globe thanks to the speed in which it takes catwalk trends and converts them into affordable high street fare.

Capas Seseña, C/ Santa Cruz, 23 legendary Spanish purveyor of fine capes for men and women

Casa de Libro, Gran Via 29 excellent bookstore for English and Spanish language books. Gran Via is the flagship, smaller branches elsewhere in the city.

De Flamenco, C/ Arenal 9 flamenco superstore for music, clothes, shoes, fans – the lot. They also publish a Flamenco magazine and have an impressive flamenco portal at www.deflamenco.com.

H&M, Gran Via 32 Swedish-based competitor to Zara, offering cheap and disposable fashion, again with outlets all over the city

Oysho, C/ Carretas 27 Lolitaesque clothing for women, girls and babies

Pull and Bear, C/ Carretas 23 Pull and Bear successfully targets a slightly dressed down clientele than its better known sibling Zara

Salvador Bachiller, C/ Alcalá 151 a small trek to the east of the centre, this is the place for traditional Spanish leatherware, or check out the smaller shop in Malasaña

Stradivarius, Gran Via 30 another in the Zara stable, Stradivarius offers a hipper edge in its womenswear

CHUECA

Madrid's gay district is brimming with small, trendy boutiques, mainly for men. Prices vary and there are some particularly good-value vintage stores and seconds shops selling designer clothes at discount prices. It's a great place to go for club-wear, and styles range from the plain t-shirt to the positively outrageous. In Chueca you'll find a plethora of shoe shops, particularly in Calle Augusto Figueroa, which is lined with one after another. Most shops close here between 2pm and 5pm, but there are plenty of cafés in which to while away the hours until opening time.

Calle Fuencarral

Adidas sports and casual wear and trainers

Billabong Aussie surf wear

Blanco pop-inspired, colourful and wearable women's fashion from established Spanish label

Camper ubiquitous Spanish trainer and shoe brand
Desigual excellent brand of Spanish streetwear
Diesel market leading quirky casual wear with fabulous jeans – also on C/ Serrano in Salamanca
G Star last word in denim designed to dress down
Gas upmarket denim and more
Hoss affordable, smart and trendy womenswear
Jack & Jones jeans and Ts at reasonable price
Kiehls New York's finest products in Madrid
Levis denim and more
MAC stylish and continually in vogue selection of make-up and other related products
Mango Spanish high-street brand
Miss Sixty/Energie casual and club wear
Muji the Japanese 'no brand' brand for fashion and home accessories
Oneill surf and sports wear and accessories
Pepe Jeans denim and more
Puma sports and casual wear and trainers
Replay funky ensati street and casual wear
Rip Curl surf wear and accessories
Sisley Benetton's more preppy sister brand

Calle Hortaleza

Cascanueves funky, clubby gear for men and women
Compañia Multihispana showcases many up and coming young Spanish designers
Coorleones sip a coffee while you browse many famous and less well-known designer labels under one roof, including Calvin Klein, Auslander, Lagerfeld and Antik denim
Fuku ultra cool Japanese designs – Ts, bags and motorbike helmets, among other accessories

Calle Piamonte

Amore & Psique elegant, contemporary men's and women's fashions
Expresion Negra Afro-inspired art, fashion and accessories. Some great things here.

Las Bailarinas de Monica un, hand-finished and quirky women's shoes by shop owner Monica Garcia

Martel Kee, C/ Piamonte 15 womenswear from French Connection and Replay, while the C/ Barquillo store is for Diesel and Paul Smith, as well as carrying lines for kids

Piamonte well-established store selling clothing and accessories to the hip crowds of Chueca

Bless, C/ Santa Bárbara 11 womenswear and accessories from brands such as IKKS, BOBA and Firetrap, Bless also carries plenty of shoes.

Callate la Boca, C/ Barquillo 24 funky cool prints on anything from Ts to bags via mugs… Great for fans of Paul Frank and Keith Haring

Carhartt, C/ Augusto Figueroa 3 perennially hip and hard-wearing urban street wear

L'Habilleur, Plaza de Chueca 8 long-standing store stocks current lines from top designers, as well as specializing in end of season bargains for men and women. They also offer a new personal shopper service.

Isolee, C/ Infantas 19 fashion, lifestyle, deli, café, bar, restaurant – you name it, Isolee has it in uber-cool form (also see SNACK)

KTW, C/ Infantas 14 modern shoes and espadrilles, which have added a splash of colour to the traditional Spanish footwear

Lotta, C/ Hernán Cortés 9 compact shop is run by a Swedish expat who is doing her best to implant the concept of vintage clothing in Spain, a country not famed for its willingness to wear second-hand clobber. If you don't see what you're after, be sure to ask for a peek at the stock not on display.

Plaisir Gourmet SL, C/ Gravina 1 excellent international deli for mouth-watering foodie gifts

Suite, C/ Augusto Figueroa 16 arguably the most eye-catching of the many shoe outlets on Augusto Figueroa, sells funky footwear from Ensati and Spanish shoe designers for both men and women.

Trash, C/ Augusto Figueroa 3 skatewear and other street fashion

Vol de Nuit, C/ San Tomé 4 eclectic mix of slightly bohemian gifts, lifestyle, shoes, clothing and accessories

Yube, C/ Fernando VI 23 run by two young entrepeneurs who regularly travel to Milan, Paris and New York to bring the latest fashions to the

Spanish capital. Catering to men and women, the labels on offer here include Paul Smith, Fred Perry, Chloe, Gold Hawk and James Perse.

MALASAÑA

For grungy, alternative fashion and good-value clubwear, head to Malasaña. There's no main shopping street so you'll have to explore its narrow streets and lanes to discover its little boutique stores and cafés. Most are independently owned and therefore close between 2pm and 5pm. Malasaña also boasts some funky little record shops where you might pick up some rare imported labels.

Chido Güey, Corredera Baja de San Pablo 26 Mexican street style and pop culture in this amazing shop that sells, among many other things, some of the hippest Ts and bags in town and the ultimate kitsch accessory – Mexican wrestling masks

Converse Deportes Paz, C/ Pez 23 one-stop Converse shop is totally dedicated to Converse sneakers, including hard-to-find editions and a complete range of accessories

Custo Barcelona, C/ Fuencarral 29 this iconic brand, one of Barcelona's most famous exports, has invaded Madrid, opening up five stores in the capital. Their use of colour combinations and printed patterns keep the customers flocking in, as does the excellent presentation in each store.

Deli Room, C/ De Santa Bárbara 4 collection of hip, up-and-coming young designers

Gildas, Corredera Alta de San Pablo 32 as well as producing their own line of clothing, the team at Gildas will also knock up an original design for you. Just explain what you're after and they'll get on the case – you can even take in old favourites for renovation.

Knight Comics, C/ Pez 2 one of the best of Malasaña's many comic book shops

La Tipo, C/ Conde del Duque, 7 cool t-shirts, shirts and aprons with fun n funky and ever so slightly subversive designs

Level Records, C/ Divino Pastor 3 one thing that Malasaña has plenty of is vinyl stores, which cater to all DJ tastes. Level records is one of the most established, you can pick up plenty of national product and imports too.

Lost People, C/ de Santa Bárbara 6   a collective for up and coming Spanish designers

Mint Marché, C/ Conde Duque 14   womenswear with a pedigree, the owners act as distributors and agents for nearby Sportivo, a favourite men's store in the city. The onus is on Parisian fashions, with a good selection of independent labels and an plentiful range of accessories.

Otaku Center, C/ Palma, 73   curious manga and modern Japanese lifestyle shop featuring an extraordinary selection of figurines, books, DVDs etc. and a back lounge with a semi-permanent dance game set up. 'All of Japan in Madrid' as their card states…

Salvador Bachiller, C/ Alberto Aguilera 54   the ultimate traditional Spanish leather accessory store – wallets, bags, gloves etc.

Snapo, C/ Espíritu Santo 5   streetwear with plenty of hoodies, hats and t-shirts on offer for the unisex youth of Malasaña. There are also plenty of badges, bags, hats and even punk-rock records to choose from.

Trendy Tube, C/ Corredera Baja de San Pablo 46   interesting shop, unusually for Madrid, featuring the work of up and coming UK designers

Shopping List

play...

With Madrid's summer temperatures soaring into the late 30s and the nightlife continuing well into the early hours, you might be tempted to pass your time here at a more leisurely pace. However, if you decide you want a more active break, you'll find the city has many sporting amenities. You only have to go to El Retiro park in the evenings to see plenty of Madrileños are keen to keep fit. Joggers, cyclists, roller-bladers and speed-walkers mingle with those who prefer just to stroll or sit on benches soaking up the glory of the evening sunshine.

Madrid is home to one of the world's most famous football clubs, Real Madrid, which also boasts one of the world's most impressive stadiums, the Santiago Bernabéu. While the era of the *galácticos* may be over, the team is still one of the most successful in Europe, which means that getting hold of tickets can be pretty tricky, but you should feel honour bound to try. Failing that Madrid has three other excellent teams, Atlético, Getafe and Rayo Vallecano. For a really atmospheric encounter get hold of some tickets for the Atlético–Real derby.

Alternatively, why not take in a more traditionally Spanish event at Las Ventas bullfighting ring? Bullfighting has become a multi-million euro business and employs around half a million Spaniards. Although this blood-letting will not

appeal to some, a *corrida* is actually an incredibly graceful experience with a balletic interplay between matador and bull. The inevitable denouement will shock, particularly as the bull is dragged out of the ring, but it is an experience everyone should enjoy once – at least to be able then to have an informed opinion on the subject.

If being cooped up in a city is not quite your cup of tea, then feel free to explore the beautiful mountains that surround Madrid. One can hire a horse or a mountain bike, head out into the Sierra mountains, and discover the natural fauna and flora – or just enjoy some exhilarating thrills and spills. For those interested in field sports there are some fantastic opportunities to shoot partridge in the surrounding hills; these trips should be organized in advance from the UK.

Madrid has come on in leaps and bounds in terms of spas in recent years, with new centres seemingly opening every month or so. Of particular note for their central location are the Medina baths, in Calle Atocha, which are based on the traditional Arabic concept of a hammam.

BULLFIGHTING

Top matadors are among the highest-paid entertainers in the world and can earn over €120,000 a day. In the last few years, bullfighting has grown in popularity and has become more fashionable, despite opposition from animal welfare groups. It is not regarded as a sport, however. It is a theatrical experience rather than a competition between man and bull. To the Spanish, it is a celebration of death: having lived for at least four years on the country's finest pastures, the bull finally gets his 'day of glory'. The season lasts from March to October and times of fights vary. Beer and soft drinks are sold inside and you can choose from seats in the sun or in the shade.

Plaza de Toros de Las Ventas, C/ Alcala 237, Madrid
Tel: 91 726 48 00/356 22 00 www.las-ventas.com
Open: 10am–2pm, 5–8pm Thurs–Sun. Closed November–February.

As this is probably the most impressive bullring in the world, with a 23,000 capacity, there's no better place to witness a bullfight; these are held every Sunday, usually at 7pm, but sometimes at 5pm. During the Feria de San Isidro, from mid-May to early June, and the Feria de Otoño, starting in late September, fights are held every day. Tickets go on sale three days before each event, but tickets for the San Isidro are usually reserved long in advance by season-ticket holders. By law, 1,000 tickets must be held back to go on sale at 10am on the morning of the fight, but there are very long queues for these. Front-row seats in the shade cost around €100, mid-range seats around €25 and gallery seats in the sun as little as €3.50. You can rent a cushion for extra comfort.

The following agents are worth a try for tickets, although they charge a 20% commission: La Central (tel: 91 522 59 46); La Oreja de Oro (tel: 91 531 33 66); La Taurina (tel: 91 369 47 56)

CYCLING

While Madrid authorities are gradually installing more and more cycle lanes, the city remains somewhat risky for bike-lovers, with aggressive motorists in particular posing dangers for those on two wheels. However, the wilderness of the Casa de Campo is great for mountain biking, while the Retiro is good for a short, easy ride. There are several companies in Madrid running mountain-bike excursions, mainly in the Sierra mountains, and if you're here on an extended stay you might want to go off for a two-night cycling break.

Bicimania, C/ Palencia 20, Cuatro Caminos, Tetuan
Tel: 91 533 11 89   www.bicimania.com
Open: 10.30am–2pm, 5–8.30pm Mon–Fri, 10.30am–2pm Sat

Well-organized excursions are on offer here, to areas of great natural beauty, such as La Pedriza and Puerto de Navafria. You get a tour leader, insurance and a snack. Longer trips are also good value.

Bike Spain Tours, Plaza de la Villa 1, Centro
Tel: 91 559 06 53   www.bikespain.info
Open: 10am–2pm, 4–7pm. Closed Saturdays and Sundays.

Bike Spain specialize in guided tours of the Camino de Santiago, Madrid, Toledo and Granada, or if you prefer it self-guided tours, where everything is arranged for you – accommodation, luggage transfers, and, of course, the route. There's even a tour of the wine regions Rioja and Ribera, although be careful not to drink and ride.

Bravo Bike, C/ Juan Álvarez Mendizábal 19, Malasana
Tel: 91 559 55 23   www.bravobike.com
Open: 10.30am–2pm, 4.30–8pm. Closed Saturdays and Sundays.

Cycling tours with a touch of class: they include accommodation in luxury hotels and dining in top restaurants.

Calmera, C/ Atocha 98, Centro
Tel: 91 527 75 74   www.calmera.es
Open: 9.30am–1.30pm, 4.30–8pm. Closed Sunday.

Just off the Paseo del Prado this bike shop has been in operation since 1942

FOOTBALL

There are four big teams in Madrid: Getafe, Atlético Madrid and Rayo Vallecano are lesser known, while Real Madrid is, of course, by far the most famous and popular. The season runs from September to June and league matches are usually played on Saturday and Sunday evenings. Tickets cost from €15 and usually go on sale a couple of days before a match, when massive queues form outside the box offices.

Atlético de Madrid, Estadio Vicente Calderon, Paseo de la Virgen del Puerto 67, Madrid
Tel: 91 366 47 07   www.clubatleticodemadrid.com

If you can, get tickets for the Atlético–Real derby – it is an intensely passionate affair. Forget Real Madrid–Barcelona – this is when the real handbags come out! Atlético won't be at their historic stadium for much longer, as they are moving to La Peineta Olympic stadium come 2010.

Getafe CF, Avda Teresa de Calcuta s/n, Getafe
Tel: 91 695 97 71   www.getafecf.com

Previously coached by Bernd Schuster, who is now at the helm at Real Madrid, this club finds its home in one of the southern suburbs of the city. The team is currently in the *Primera*, and as well as an army of home-grown fans, enjoys support throughout the world.

Rayo Vallecano, Estadio de Maria Teresa Riverio, Avenida Payaso Fofo, Madrid
Tel: 91 478 22 53   www.rayovallecano.es

This club has a faithful following in its home, the blue-collar neighbourhood of Vallecas. They are fairly firmly stuck in the second division, but have had past glories such as reaching the UEFA cup quarter finals back in 2001.

Real Madrid, Estadio Santiago Bernabéu, Avenida de Concha Espina, Madrid
Tel: 91 398 43 00/90 227 17 08   www.realmadrid.com

Their superstar players, such as Ronaldo, Beckham and Zidane, may be long gone, but a trip to Real Madrid still ensures a chance to watch some of the world's finest footballers. Even if you don't make it to a match, the guided tour of the stadium itself is excellent – particularly of their trophy room. Real Madrid has a telephone booking system through the bank Caja Madrid (tel: 90 232 43 24), but you'll still have to queue to collect your tickets. The Bernabéu is one of Madrid's largest stadiums, but although it holds up to 75,000 spectators, it is surprisingly easy to get in and out. It is best to go for the tickets that cost between €20 and €30 in the middle tier.

GOLF

Seve Ballesteros and Sergio Garcia have put Spain firmly on the golfing map. There are some magnificent public and private courses dotted around the city, but they can get rather busy at weekends, so check ahead for availability.

Club de Campo Villa de Madrid, Carretera de Castilla
Tel: 91 550 08 40   www.clubvillademadrid.com
Open: daily, 8am–10pm

An expensive and difficult course, designed by Javier Arana and Seve Ballesteros. This club also boasts squash and tennis courts, clay pigeon and range shooting, hockey pitches, polo facilities, horse-riding and swimming.

Golf Olivar de la Hinojosa, Avenida de Dublín, Campo de las Naciones.
Tel: 91 721 18 89   www.golfolivar.com
Open: daily, 8.30am–8pm

A public facility offering both golf and tennis. There are two courses, one 18-hole and one nine-hole, where rounds cost from €18.50 depending on how many holes you play.

Golf Park, Avda de Europa 10, Parque Empresarial de la Moraleja, Alcobendas
Tel: 91 661 44 44   www.golfpark.es
Open: daily, 10am (9am Sat/Sun)–10.30pm

A nine-hole driving range just outside the city on the N-1 road to Burgos. Here you can play a round for €21 or pay €2.40 for a bucket of 30 balls on the driving range.

HORSE-RIDING

Madrid is located on a dry plateau in the mountains of central Spain, there-fore if you do take time to get out of the city the best and quickest way to explore the surrounding countryside is on horseback. The surrounding scenery is simply stunning and you can relive some of your spaghetti Western fantasies as Sergio Leone shot his movies in Spain.

Indiana Parque Recreativo Natural, Apdo Correos 32, San Martin de Valdeiglesias
Tel: 91 861 27 99 www.indiana-sl.com
Open: daily, 9am–8pm

Experienced riders can trek across rivers and up mountains. There's also a school for beginners as well as a chance to try climbing, archery and canoeing.

Las Palomas, Club H'pico, Carretera de Colmenar Viejo
Tel: 90 872 87 95/91 803 31 76
Open: 10am–2pm and 5–7pm. Closed Mondays.

Riding for all levels just a 30km drive from the city.

SHOOTING & HUNTING

The red-legged partridge is a game bird that is noted for its speed and movement. Guns from around the world descend on Spain during the season (mid-September to the end of February) to try their luck. One can either dedicate a weekend to it or simply take a day out and enjoy the country air and the sport.

La Nava, Casas de Monteagu, Almuradiel
Tel: 91 564 57 30 www.lanava.net

A 25,000 hectare estate just off the E5 and a couple of hours from Madrid is La Nava, run by Roberto Medem; the birds fly seriously hard and fast and are more than a match for most guns. For those with their own plane the estate has its own strip and for those not shooting the extremely comfortable lodge and pool are perfect. The food is fantastic and the service impeccable.

The Partridge Club
Tel: (+44) 7000 868 935 www.partridgeclub.com

A British organization that lets out days that are surplus to their members' requirements. Located just over 30km south-east of Madrid, this private hunting estate specializes in high valleys and therefore some really testing birds.

SPAS AND HAMMAMS

In a marked switch from just a few years ago, Madrid is now awash with top-class spas and beauty centres, many of them drawing on the Arabic roots of the city for inspiration – Madrid, after all, is named after the Arabic word *mayrit*, meaning many springs.

Chi Spa, Conde de Aranda 6, Salamanca
Tel: 91 578 13 40 www.thechispa.com
Open: 10am–9pm Mon–Fri; 10am–6pm Sat. Closed Sundays.

One of Madrid's chicest spas, Chi opened in 2003 to much acclaim. This small and welcoming spa is in the heart of Salamanca, and, as you can guess from the name, has an Oriental theme. The treatments on offers range from facials to massages and even a full-body waxing for men, especially useful for the more hirsuite Spanish. Slippers, bathrobes, towels and a private locker are provided, and consultants are on hand to advise on treatments. Cash tips are expected.

City Yoga, Calle Los Artistas 43, Madrid
Tel: 91 553 47 51 www.city-yoga.com
Open: daily, 10am–10pm

If you are in need of stretching, tight muscles and a mysteriously delicious peace of mind City Yoga has recently opened four floors of karma in the heart of a busy metropolis. The centre offers Iyengar, Vinyasa, Kundalini, Hatha yoga plus pre and post natal yoga. Spacious rooms allow natural sunlight and a very comfortable atmosphere designed to cater for every age and fitness level. A natural therapy section provides a range of massage and natural healing such as Shiatsu or Indian Head massage and a juice bar serves healthy snacks. A well-stocked bookshop sells Spanish and English publications and yoga clothing from the Prana range.

Medina Mayrit Arabic Baths, C/ Atocha 14, Centro
Tel: 90 233 33 34 www.medinamayrit.com
Open: daily, 10am–noon, 2–4pm, 6–8pm

Located in a stunning 100-year-old cistern just off the Plaza Mayor, these authentic Arabic baths offer two-hour sessions throughout the day. Bathers can dip in and out of cold, warm and hot baths, and perhaps opt for a 15-minute aromatherapy or exfoliating massage as well. For a complete hammam circuit you must allow 90 minutes. The baths are popular with couples and groups, and bookings are a must – and do remember to bring a proper swimming costume.

02 Wellness Centre, C/ Don Ramón de la Cruz 33, Salamanca
Tel: 91 431 40 43 www.o2centrowellness.com
Open: daily, 7am–11pm

With the emphasis, unsurprisingly on 'Wellness' this expanding chain is perfect for those who delight in everythig esoteric from the safety and comfort of modern, clean surrounds. The O2 group offer everything from yoga, tai chi and a fitness centre, but also has a beauty centre, cafe and a laundry service.

Spa Relajarse, C/ Barquillo, 43, Chueca
Tel: 91 308 61 48 www.sparelajarse.com
Open: 11am–11pm Mon–Sat; 1pm–1am Sun

At another orientally themed health spa you can also enjoy some oxygentherapy, a turkish bath, a revitalizing facial or a decent massage as well as a bite at the sushi bar to top it all off.

SWIMMING

There are several open-air pools in Madrid, but unfortunately they are only open from June until September, despite the sometimes soaring temperatures in surrounding months. Public pools each have their own pricing and ticket system and you will need a swimming cap if entering an indoor pool. The most popular pools are in the Casa de Campo (see below).

Hotel Emperador, Gran Via 53, Centro
Tel: 91 547 28 00
Open: 11am–9pm daily, June–September

The rooftop pool at this hotel is open to non-guests for a fee of around €24. It has stunning city views and is a decent size.

Piscinas Casa de Campo, Avenida del Ángel
Tel: 91 463 00 50
Open: daily, 10.30am–8pm May–September

There are three open-air pools here, one Olympic-sized, one for children and one intermediate. They get very crowded at weekends but are fairly quiet during the week. At certain times they are closed off for OAPs or particular activities, so it's best to call beforehand to make sure they are open. Facilities also include changing-rooms, cafés and sunbathing areas. Topless sunbathing is allowed, and there is an informal gay area.

TENNIS

Owing to the climate and a propensity for warm springs and autumns, tennis is a popular sport in the Spanish capital. With the success of Rafa Nadal, Spain is riding high in the tennis world. Municipal *polideportivos* can be rented by the hour, but you have to bring your own equipment. Courts can be found at most of the city-run swimming-pool complexes.

Tenis Casa de Campo, Casa de Campo
Tel: 91 464 91 67

This complex, close to the boating lake, has 15 courts and floodlighting. It's the best-run public court and costs less than €5 for an hour.

TOURS

Sometimes the best way to really see a city is to take a view through someone else's eyes. We don't advocate the usual herd mentality of aimlessly following shouty women, with their umbrellas held aloft like beacons in the night, instead relying on a more graceful approach.

Letango Tours

Tel: 91 369 47 52 or 655 818 740 (mobile) www.letango.com

A licensed travel agency and tour operator in Madrid, Letango specializes in day tours, excursions outside the city, and longer tours for smaller or larger groups that will help you get really close to the local flavour and culture. Carlos Galvin, a native of Madrid, has 10 years of experience showing visitors the best of what his city has to offer. He and his American wife Jennifer run the tours. In addition to walking and museum tours, Letango's culinary tour will introduce you to some centuries old Madrileño specialities as well as offering some invaluable help in how to approach the fast-paced tapas scene in some of the hottest bars in Madrid. A three hour tour costs €95 per person, minimum of two people. See Letango's website for more info on services and prices including hotel bookings, itineraries and walking tours all over.

Activity schedule

info...

DANGERS

Pickpockets at the Rastro market and around Puerta del Sol are the biggest
dangers in Madrid. Tourists are prime targets, so try not to look like one and
keep a tight hold on your bags and cameras. If you are wandering the dark
streets of Malasaña, Chueca or La Latina in the early hours of the morning it
always pays to be careful as muggings are increasingly commonplace. Try and
keep to the lighter, brighter streets or just grab a taxi to get around. Groups of
young children will sometimes try to get your attention by holding up a piece
of paper while you are sitting at a terrace bar. Watch your belongings, as they
are most likely trying to distract you while they grab whatever's sitting on the
table.

PUBLIC TRANSPORT

Madrid's metro is quick, clean, easy to navigate and ridiculously cheap. For a
weekend stay, it's best to buy a ticket for 10 journeys (€6.15), which can be
used on the metro and the buses. It doesn't matter how long the 10 journeys
are, your ticket is still valid on the lines in the centre. Two people can share the
ticket simply by passing it back when going through the ticket barriers. Each
time the ticket passes through, a tiny mark is made on the back and the number of remaining journeys is displayed on the ticket barrier, so you can keep
track of how many trips you have left to make. There is no collection of tickets
as you exit the station. On some platforms, boards display how long it has been
since the last train departed, while on others they show how long you will have
to wait for the next. If you're travelling to or from the airport, you will need to
buy a supplementary ticket, which costs €1. Buses in Madrid are frequent and
numerous, although the heavy traffic they often get caught in can make journeys
very slow. After the Metro stops running at weekends (at around 1.30am), a
night bus service runs the routes of the main Metro lines until the early hours
of the morning.

SMOKING

Smoking is a major pastime in Spain, and the introduction of a smoking ban has
done little to curb that. In Madrid, bars of under 100 square metres can choose

whether or not to ban smoking. Most bars are, of course, under this size, so it is still normal for people to light up. Public buildings are now a no-no for the smoker, however, meaning that – thankfully – your bank teller is no longer likely to blow smoke in your face as he or she cashes up your travellers' cheques.

TAXIS

Taxis are plentiful in Madrid and you usually won't have to wait more than a couple of minutes for one. The only exception is when it's raining or late at night in the main bar and nightclub areas. You'll know if it's free if it has a 'Libre' sign behind the windscreen and a green light on the roof. If the driver is also displaying a sign with a district written in red, this means he is on his way home and is not obliged to take you if it is not on his route. Taxi ranks are marked with a blue Taxi sign. Drivers won't always speak English, but are generally good at knowing their way around – especially since the advent of GPS. A taxi from the airport to the city centre will cost around €20–25 including a €5 supplement. There are also small supplements for baggage and for trips on Sundays. Go to the official rank outside the arrivals area, and ignore anyone who approaches you along the way.

For a reputable taxi service, tel: 91 447 32 32 or 91 371 21 31

TELEPHONES

All the telephone numbers in this guide are without the international code. To call from the UK, dial 00 34 before the Madrid code 91. Remember to have your international option activated on your mobile phone. Rates will vary.

TIPPING

There are no hard and fast rules with tipping and locals tend to tip very little. However, visitors are generally expected to tip 5–10% to waiters in restaurants, and maybe to leave a few cents in a bar. It's also customary to give small tips to hotel porters and lavatory attendants and to round up the fare or leave around 5% for taxi drivers.

Hg2 Madrid

index